It Takes a Village

SHAKTI MEHTA

ISBN
Paperback: 979-8-89544-801-4
Hardcase: 979-8-89588-391-4

The real-life story of 3 Dwarfs having physical disabilities with their Father "a Giant of a Man" (literally and figuratively) and a supportive Mother.

Their Approach towards life was "Never Say Die!"

Contents

Preface

The idea of writing this book was seeded when our father switched off the television midway while watching the movie "Taare Zameen Par". This is a heart-wrenching movie about a differently abled boy who is scorned by everyone except the hero of the movie. The hero a teacher, who recognizes his innate talent and devotes his time to developing it in the boy, and our father unable to bear it, switches the TV off.

Our first thought when our father did that was that it was logical. Being a parent of three differently abled children, we thought, he must be distressed by the experience of the boy and unable to bear the trauma, he switched it off.

We could not have been more off the mark!

"The world isn't half as bad as these guys have made it out to be", Dad said. "Sure, there would be a few people who are unable to accept you as you are, but a large majority of people would like to walk an extra mile to help you. This movie unfortunately focuses only on the first type and by doing that, demeans the entire world."

This resonated with what we had always been taught. Our parents had always talked to us about recognizing the good that people had done for us and being grateful for all they had done. They had also told us that we were bound to meet people who would either ignore us or seek to demean us, but it was our job to remember the good folks and ignore the rest.

This crisp summary of societal behaviour is what prompted us to think about penning our experiences and how virtually the whole society around us helped us meet our challenging life head-on. Accepting our limitations (we would have been stupid not to) and yet, determined to never let them limit our dreams and ambitions.

Subsequently, many friends, family members, and well-wishers suggested to us that we must write our memoirs so that others could benefit from it.

So, here is a humble attempt to present to you, the reader, some of the key highlights of what transpired in our lives. This is not a memoir in the true sense of the word as we have tried to focus only on what we felt to be relevant. And yet, it does broadly capture the significant milestones of our lives.

Memory, it is said, is not always about what happened but often a reconstructed version of what our brain wants us to believe what happened. From that point of view, if there is any inaccuracy, the blame is entirely on me who is writing on behalf of all five of us.

Would it be?
Would it not be...?

It was the early morning of 4th of July 1965. In Nanavati Hospital at Vile Parle (West), a suburb of Mumbai, there was an air of hope accompanied by dread and fear, a very big FEAR. Yashodhara was to deliver her third child. The first TWO were short in height and were physically challenged.

She delivered a baby boy and when the nurse handed over that child to her, Yashodhara looked at him and lamented, pleaded to the doctor....

PLEASE KILL HIM, what will he do? How will he survive? ....

Chapter 1

The Family of Five

The first child of Chandraketu (Pappa) and Yashodhara (Mummy) was a daughter named Shubhani (fondly, we at home, and people close to us call her Chhuma). Though Shubhani was born with a congenital disability and was short of build, this was taken as a freak event. And why not? Pappa was a giant of a man who stood at 6 feet 2 inches. By qualification, he was a Mechanical and Electrical Engineer. He was also a very good sportsman and had a great sense of humour.

Mummy was a homemaker and was 5 feet 4 inches tall, was aggressive by nature, and could not tolerate misbehaviour or injustice. She would immediately respond to that. Medically, both of them were normal and no person in their families had any deformity. Doctors had told Pappa and Mummy that Shubhani would not be able to walk (a few years later they were proven wrong).

The second child was a boy (Shakti), younger than Shubhani by 14 months. As compared to Shubhani, I looked healthier. Even though I was born with congenital deformities, the deformities showed true colour as I grew up. Till I was 6 years old, I looked quite normal except for being short of build.

This improvement in the second child gave hope to the doctors, Pappa, and Mummy that perhaps the third child could be normal. Having a normal child was very important for Pappa and Mummy, as they felt that he/she could take care of Shubhani and me when the need arose.

As a precaution, Mummy was treated by one of the leading gynaecologists of Mumbai and after a period of 4 years, they decided to go for the third child. To their shock and horror, Maulik, when born, had the most severe deformities of the three siblings. In this situation, Mummy could simply not stop herself from pleading with the doctor to kill him.

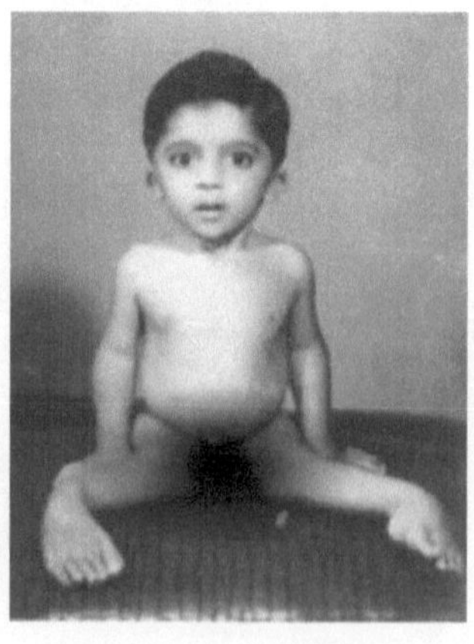

In medical terms, it is called Arthrogryposis Multiplex Congenita (AMC). If the deformities were to be described in layman's language, then for Shubhani it would be: no knee caps, so legs do not bend; legs from the knee joint move outwards; improper elbow joint, so hands do not get stretched straight; and height of three feet. For Shakti, it would be: improper elbow joint, so hands do not get stretched straight; curved spinal cord; knock knees; and height of about four feet. For Maulik, it would be: no knee caps, so legs do not bend; legs from the knee joint move outwards (almost like a frog); curved spinal cord; improper elbow joint, so hands do not get stretched straight; and height of about three feet and ten inches.

What do we call, their Struggle or their Fight?

It is difficult to say exactly whether this can be considered a struggle or a fight, but Pappa and Mummy decided that they had a challenge on hand and they would meet it head-on....

Under these circumstances, it is very likely that a person can either start hating God or simply surrender to Him and become totally religious. But surprisingly, Pappa and Mummy could maintain that fine balance. They did not hate God and never complained to Him. In fact, they always strongly believed and maintained that whenever they needed help, He would be there and would always help even without asking.

To live with such grace and poise amidst such difficult conditions might have been very difficult, but it proved to be very effective.

Two good things followed. Because all three of us had deformities, there was no discrimination possible when it came to handling us. Secondly, and more importantly, Pappa and Mummy started dealing with us as if we were normal children.

These two things made a very big difference in the lives of Shubhani, Maulik, and me as we realized that our responsibilities were equal and we would be treated for almost everything like any other child in other families.

One major reason for Shubhani, Maulik, and I never having a problem with an inferiority complex was the wonderful upbringing by our parents. Instead of having any grudge against us, they, in fact, loved us and were very possessive about us.

Some of the questions that Pappa and Mummy always had in the back of their minds were:

- About our education
- How will we earn our livelihood?
- Our acceptability by society at large
- Our marriage
- Who will take care of them when they grow old?
- Who will take care of the three of us when they are not there?

There were no immediate answers. The only clear thing was that for the three of us, good education was the only way to earn our livelihood. The other questions were buried down somewhere, hoping to get some answers in the future.

Even though the weight of the responsibility for Pappa and Mummy was very heavy, the atmosphere at home was not at all heavy.

Pappa always believed that whatever has happened, has happened. You cannot undo it. Think about what best can be done from that point onwards and do that wholeheartedly. Mummy had emphasised that no matter what happens, even if the entire world turns against us, we five should remain firm in our relationship.

"A true and genuine relationship develops not because of money or power that you have but is because of your good and transparent behaviour and as Osho says if you want that world should love you then the first condition is that you must love yourself"

Chapter 2

Early Upbringing

We get settled in Mumbai

Pappa came to Mumbai for his company's work, the understanding was that after the assignment was over, he would return to Gujarat. Since Pappa was expected to be in Mumbai only for a short time, he stayed at Partner's house. 'Partner' was one of his friends and his roommate in the hostel during college days, and both addressed each other as 'Partner'. This closeness with each other continued, and both addressed each other as "Partner" till the end.

After the assignment was over, the management of the company felt that Pappa should be stationed in Mumbai. Pappa told the promoter of that company that he did not have money even to pay the deposit for the house. The promoter told the accountant to give money to Pappa to pay the deposit of the house. Pappa selected a house at Irla (Vile Parle West) and paid the deposit; the year was 1962.

The location of our house played a very important role in our life as schools, colleges, and bus stops were very near to our house. As Pappa did not have a sister, Partner's sister started tying Rakhi to him, and this practice also continued till the end. Her husband was a doctor. Apart from being our family doctor, he was a family friend too. We sought his advice for many tricky questions as he was a person who would not tell us what we liked but what was right.

In a very short period, we got admitted into their group of families and friends. This was mainly on account of Pappa's great sense of humour and his jovial nature. He cracked jokes on the spur of the moment, and with him around, the atmosphere was always joyful. The group used to go on short weekend trips, and we were always a part of that. In retrospect, these trips had a great impact on the personality of all three of us as in the school we always had something to boast about on Mondays. We would describe to the other children and teachers about the weekend experience. This elevated us to a level where, instead of us feeling low, the other people were envious of us.

How Pappa And Mummy Treated And Taught Us

Our family had a very humble beginning. Financially, we were not strong, but the quality of life at home was very interesting. Despite the problems that we faced and an uncertain future, each member of the family was always smiling, and we had a lot of fun. The atmosphere at home was so relaxing that many of our relatives and friends used to come to our house and would say without hesitation that, as they were stressed, they decided to come to our place to get rid of their tension.

We had a bicycle on which Pappa and Mummy would take us for a ride. Pappa and Mummy would walk, and we would be on the bicycle. During those rides, they would also teach us about how to remain positive. This was done in such a subtle manner that we never felt they were preaching.

Some very important messages which were conveyed to us during some of those rides:

- *They will not be able to create a different world for us. The world is what it is and we will have to find our way in this very world*

- *Most of the people in this world are good and we must learn to ignore the rest of the people*

- *We should not hesitate to seek help from others but at the same time we should do so only when it is necessary*

I have a very fond memory of such walks. On some occasions, I also would be walking with Mummy and Pappa. Having walked some distance, when I used to get tired and would tell Pappa about it, Pappa would say, "Dikra, if you are tired, then let us walk slowly till we cross the fifth lamp post, after that, we decide what has to be done." We three then would count the lamp posts. As we walked further, I would simply forget I was tired! After reaching the fifth lamp post, he would ask me to rest for a while, and then again, we would move ahead and reach our destination! This was what our father was, a great motivator who used to introduce us to our own hidden capacity!

The very important lesson was: *"The entire job may look very difficult, but when broken up into parts, going from one milestone to the next one with determination, most of the time you will be able to complete it."*

Initial Years of Our Upbringing

Pappa used to change companies as frequently as we changed clothes (including two stints as a professor at VJTI and Sardar Patel College, very reputed engineering colleges in Mumbai in those years). Finally, he joined a company in Mumbai where he stayed until his retirement.

One very important revenue stream of that company was developing manufacturing facilities producing agro-chemicals on a turnkey basis. Pappa was heading this activity and so had to be at the manufacturing site for long periods, during which he would be away from the family. Despite that, he remained in touch with us by way of letters (the telephone then was a luxury and would take hours to get connected). These letters were so well written that we would eagerly wait for his letters.

Whenever he came back, he would ensure that he spent enough time with us and Mummy. He also had that knack for giving "surprises". He would return from the office and tell us, "Let us go for a movie," or he would take us to a place where he would play cricket with us. He brought home our first car on the 1st of April, Fools' Day. We were not ready to believe it until we saw it, and he took us to Juhu Beach.

He was never "tired," and this trait of "not getting tired" remained till his last breath. Mentally and physically, he was so strong that he would take all three of us even on public transport. He was always on the lookout for something that would either entertain us or improve our knowledge. One more thing was that he would try his best to take us to places where he had gone and had found interesting.

In our community, all marriages would take place at Bhavnagar (our native place). In one of the marriages that the entire family attended, while returning, Mummy quietly took me to the corner of the other room and said, "Don't tell anyone, but Pappa has booked flight tickets for us; we are not returning by train."

In those days, flying was a super luxury! The joy and the pride of that flight while entering the aircraft, the churning in the stomach when the aircraft lifted itself up, the amusement when you looked down, and the buildings started becoming small, the feeling of bumps when we were passing through the cloud. Pappa was explaining to us how the pilot, through the movement of wings, was controlling these things. The thrill cannot be explained; it can only be experienced!

On every vacation, an invitation for some marriage or the other would always be there. Our grandparents would ask Pappa to attend all the marriages with all of us as an invitation in those days always meant "with family." Pappa once told our grandmother politely, "When I come to Bhavnagar to attend a marriage with family, for me it is a big effort. Also, as all marriages are the same, my children will not see anything else in life. Instead, I would like to take them to different places and would rather put my effort into that." That idea was not liked by my grandparents, but there was no room for argument.

The promoters of the company where Pappa worked were down-to-earth, humble, and had a very humane approach towards all the employees and their families. They had a very high regard for Pappa and special love and affection for the three of us. For one of the summer vacations that was approaching, Pappa applied for leave. The Managing Director (MD) asked him where he was planning to take the family for the vacation. Pappa said he had not yet decided and perhaps he would spend time with the family at home.

The MD told him that he could plan a trip to Northern India, stay at the company's guesthouse in Chandigarh, and from there visit Shimla, Kullu, and Manali. He also ensured that all the arrangements for the car and driver would be made by the company. It was a very big thing for us as we could visit three hill stations and all the prominent places of Chandigarh! The guesthouse, which was a bungalow, was no less than a resort.

In another such vacation, the stay was in the same guesthouse, and this time the places we visited were Amritsar (where we visited Jallianwala Baug, Wagah border, and Golden Temple), Delhi, and Agra (where we visited Qutub Minar, Red Fort, Taj Mahal, and Fatehpur Sikri). When we started for Fatehpur Sikri, Mummy told me that Pappa would untie a thread at Fatehpur Sikri on that day. The belief is that first, you need to tie a thread, make a wish, and untie a thread once your wish is fulfilled.

I asked her curiously, "Tell me what Pappa's wish is?" She smiled and replied, "When Pappa and I had come over here, Pappa had made a wish that he would like to bring the three of you here. It looked like a tall order then, but it is happening today!"

On successful completion of one of the projects of the company, one of the directors took Pappa and Mummy out for dinner at the Taj Hotel in Mumbai. It may not sound like a very big event today, but in those days it certainly was. While returning from that dinner, Pappa told

Mummy that one day we should bring our children to the Taj Hotel as they should have the experience of what it is like.

Both of them knew that in a way going to the Taj Hotel was not our cup of tea, but they worked out something. It was not possible to go to the restaurant where both of them had gone as three of us were minors then and that restaurant was a bar-cum-dining hall. Again, it was a surprise to us, when they said we were going to the Gateway of India to have a view of the sea which is different compared to Juhu Beach. As we were reaching Gateway of India, Pappa told the driver of the taxi to take us to the Taj Hotel. He took us to the coffee shop and ordered samosas and Fanta which we shared to minimize the bill amount. We saw Gateway of India and the rough sea from the windows of the Taj Hotel, an experience we cannot forget!

Pappa would go to great lengths to make us enjoy life like other kids. He would even bring firecrackers during Diwali. As you probably know, the real pleasure in firecrackers is to light the firecracker yourself, but after lighting, one has to come back quickly to a safe distance. Since we could not do this, Pappa would pick us up one by one, take us to the firecracker, we would light the firecracker, and Pappa would quickly bring us back.

Pappa and Mummy were not only ensuring that we were enjoying life like other kids but also preparing us to face challenges that we were likely to face in the future. One such challenge that they anticipated was cooking. They visualized that in the future there could be a situation when there would be a question about who will cook so that we three can eat. They decided to teach cooking to Shubhani when she was about twelve years old.

As Shubhani was barely three feet in height, she could not reach the gas stove as it was on a standing kitchen platform, so they brought it down, and Mummy started teaching cooking to Shubhani. Now imagine the scene: Shubhani is just three feet in height, and she is not able to bend her legs, so when she sits on the floor her legs are straight (at 180 degrees), and the length of her arms is shorter compared to other people, and they do not straighten up completely. Despite all this, she was taught cooking.

When our grandmother saw the scene, she completely disagreed with this training. She raised the point in the evening with Pappa and said we must show some pity for the plight of Shubhani and must stop this. Pappa explained to her the logic and cautioned her too that some burns and bruises would be there, but that happens to everybody, and she should not create a scene about that. He convinced her that whatever was being done was for the benefit of the three of us.

Their faith turned out to be correct as Shubhani started cooking. Their aim was that she should learn some very basic cooking, but instead, she started to cook everything, and the food was tasty. She enjoyed cooking and, most importantly, she was not unduly tired because of that. Her ability to cook helped the entire family tremendously when Mummy was not well.

The most important factor in the life of the three of us was that Pappa and Mummy were never ashamed of us. They were, in fact, very proud of us and had tremendous confidence in us. On one occasion, one of the directors of Pappa's company came to our house with his wife. They had three daughters. Pappa, Mummy, the director, and his wife, all four of them, went to Juhu Beach. Over there, the director's wife commented that she was telling her husband that they were better off compared to Pappa and Mummy as even though they did not have a son, at least they did not have children like what Pappa and Mummy have.

After returning home, Mummy told Pappa very firmly not to invite that lady again to our house as she was not interested in knowing how that lady felt about her daughters, but she was very proud of her own children. When one hears these things, one can feel a surge of blood and adrenaline rushing through the veins. These were the things that kept on reminding us that we should do so well in our lives that it would make our parents proud.

Another wonderful thing was that we would make fun of each other, but this was purely for laughter and never to insult. Because of these light moments in the family, the three of us developed the attitude where we could make fun of ourselves, laugh, and enjoy those moments, and would not feel offended unnecessarily. We would not take offense when somebody pulled our legs or made fun of us as long as it was in good taste. People really appreciated this quality.

All three of us inherited Pappa's sense of humour. Because of this sense of humour, other people always wanted us to be around.

Maulik had a hobby of solving puzzles given in Sunday's papers. The prize for that solution was that in the next Sunday's papers, they would print the name of the person who had solved the puzzle first. So, the first thing that Maulik would do on Sunday morning was to solve that puzzle. Pappa would then immediately go to Flora Fountain to hand over that solution to the office of the newspaper. Most of the time, he would be the first person to submit. Maulik's name had appeared in the newspaper many times. This was a big morale booster not only for Maulik but for the entire family.

This was at a time when Sunday was the only holiday. Even then, Pappa without fail would go to town with the puzzle solved by Maulik, whereas now most people have a holiday on Saturday and Sunday and even then, people say that they do not have time for kids.

Chapter 3

Surgeries and Schoolings

The process of consulting orthopaedic surgeons had already started, but with the birth of Maulik, it picked up momentum. Unfortunately, nobody was giving us even false hope. One of the leading orthopaedic surgeons told Pappa point-blank, "One doesn't have to feed stones, but you will have to feed your children." Imagine you go to the doctor to find a solution, and this is what he gives you as advice.

A very dear friend of Pappa was in the US, and he suggested that X-rays and other reports of Shubhani be sent to him. He consulted one of the doctors in the US, and that doctor suggested that rather than coming to the US, these reports should be shown to Dr. Katrak in Mumbai. Pappa took all of us to his clinic in Marine Lines. He examined us and suggested that first, he would like to start the surgery on Maulik. This was because he was just an infant and would get the maximum benefit from the surgery. It was decided that it would be Maulik who would first go through the surgery routine.

We stayed in Vile Parle (West) and Nanavati Hospital was very near to our residence. Shubhani and I were studying in a school which was adjacent to Nanavati Hospital. Logically, it would have been far easier if the surgeries had taken place at Nanavati Hospital. But there was one issue. Dr. Katrak resided near his clinic in Marine Lines, so he said that if surgeries were performed at Nanavati Hospital, then he could come to see Maulik only once a week. But if it were done at his nursing home, then he could visit every day.

People who know the geography of Mumbai will know how much hardship one must go through to travel from Vile Parle to Marine Lines. But Pappa and Mummy decided that Dr. Katrak attending to Maulik daily was more important, and so they decided that surgeries would be conducted at Marine Lines.

Maulik's first surgery started when he was two and a half years old and the last surgery ended when he was five. We have forgotten the number of surgeries that Maulik went through, but the number would be more than ten. At the end of the last surgery, from the looks of a frog, he was now like a human being standing on his two feet.

Very few people who are alive today know what Maulik went through during that period of surgery. After one of the surgeries, his leg had to be kept in a vertical position (at 90 degrees), so his leg was tied to the upper rod of the cradle. This was for a period of one and a half months, which was repeated at the time of the surgery of the second leg. This position remained in his mind for his entire life. Many a time, in his sleep, his leg would be at 90 degrees. We would tell him to relax. He then would adjust himself and go to sleep again.

During this period of two and a half years, he was either in plaster or was going through physiotherapy at Nanavati Hospital. One of the therapies was pouring hot wax on the legs and then allowing it to cool down. People used to gather around Maulik when they poured hot wax on his legs. But for some, even to witness that scene was not easy.

While all this was on, Shubhani and my schooling had started, and the school was in proximity to Nanavati Hospital. In the morning, Mummy had to make us ready for school, prepare tiffin for Shubhani and me, and then come to drop us at school, before we went to school, we had to ensure that Maulik went to sleep, I would softly sing a song so that he goes to sleep, sharing the responsibility came to us naturally, even in that young age we never shirked it nor were indifferent to it.

Maybe, it was the strong desire to recover from our deformities that when it came to surgery of myself and Shubhani neither I nor she were afraid of the same even after seeing all the difficulties Maulik had faced.

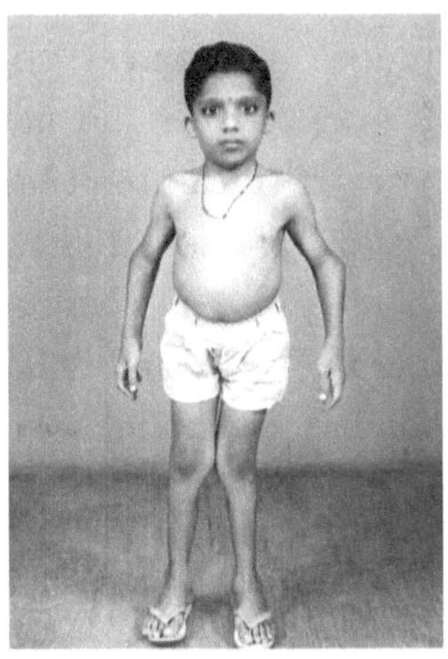

I remember very distinctly that after my surgery when I was brought out from the operation theatre and I had come out of the dizziness, I started feeling the pain in my knees where I was operated on, Pappa was sitting next to me and I told him that I was having pain and he very gently patted on the plaster at that place and asked me whether I was feeling a bit better and I said yes, today when I think about it, I realise that it was psychological but the fact is that I really felt better, this is how we felt when he was around, never worried about anything.

When Shubhani was in 2nd standard, I was in KG and my school was only for half a day. Because of this, Mummy had to go to school twice, once in the afternoon to fetch me and once in the evening to fetch Shubhani.

To avoid this, Pappa requested the principal of the school to consider admitting me to 1st standard so that Mummy could get some relief. As for Mummy, apart from all other responsibilities, one major one was to take care of Maulik. The principal agreed but with a condition that if they felt that I was not coping and was not performing well, then they would shift me back to KG. They did not transfer me back to KG.

Shubhani's Schooling

When Shubhani was born, our grandparents suggested that they would take care of her. As our grandmother did not have a daughter, this arrangement would give her the pleasure of bringing up one. So, they took Shubhani to Dhrangadra (a town in Gujarat). For Shubhani, her grandmother was like a mother, and she would address her as "Mummy" and address our real mother as "Yashoben." This equation did not change till the last. Our grandmother loved Shubhani so much that she would do everything that could make her smile.

Shubhani could not walk and had to be lifted for any movement. How it happened is not known, but one day she got up on her own and started walking. As Pappa had moved to Mumbai, Shubhani was brought to Mumbai for better education and for medical reasons. She was admitted to Nanavati School, and the principal of the school was so cooperative and concerned about her that she ensured that till the 11th standard, her classroom was always on the ground floor.

When Shubhani's surgeries started, there was a problem of her not being able to attend the classes. Pappa and Mummy went to the principal and suggested allowing them to take home the notebooks of one of the students. They would copy the lessons and give back the notebooks to the student. Pappa and Mummy would then read out the lessons to Shubhani.

In those days, there were only two exams, one was known as the terminal exam which was at the end of six months, and the other was the final exam which was at the end of the year. Since Shubhani, due to her surgeries, could not go to school, the school came up with a novel idea for conducting her exam. At the exam time, Mummy would go to school where they would hand over the question paper to her, which she would bring home. It was her responsibility to ensure that Shubhani was allowed only three hours to write the paper, and she had to ensure that Shubhani would not copy while writing the paper. There was no supervision from the school's side. They trusted us fully and never questioned anything. Shubhani cleared the exams, and this effort ensured that not a single year of her schooling was wasted.

After her surgeries, there was one major problem. Her surgeries did not give the results that Dr. Katrak was expecting. He told Pappa and Mummy that she would need crutches and would not be able to walk the way she was able to earlier. A lady doctor used to come home for her physiotherapy. She was very firm that she would not allow Shubhani to take crutches and would push her to try to walk without any support. Her perseverance finally paid off; Shubhani started walking without crutches.

This was a classic case of believing in yourself and bringing about the result with sheer determination.

Shubhani started to attend school again and cleared the SSC exam.

My Schooling

I also started my schooling at Nanavati School. The problem was that boys were allowed only till 4th standard, and from 5th standard onwards, it was a girls' high school. So, after completing the 4th standard, I had to be shifted to another school. The principal of Nanavati School suggested that I should be shifted to Sanskar Jyot as the school was very nearby, and that year was the first year of the school. I was admitted to Sanskar Jyot.

Like Nanavati School, this school was also not very big. There were no divisions, and in one class there were not more than 30 students. With the kind of fees, students were either from higher middle class or well-to-do families. Because of the small number of students in the class, there was always a one-to-one relationship between the students and the teachers. I was an above-average student; and because of my jovial nature, I was popular in the class.

After the final exam of 5th standard, during the vacation, my surgery was taken up. This surgery was to solve the problem of knock-knees. After the surgery, there was a plaster from the toe to the armpit for 45 days. For 45 days I had to sleep in one position, and all the activities were in bed. The same was the case with Shubhani and Maulik after their surgeries. Because of this long period of plaster, all the joints, starting from back to toe, are completely stiff, and one has to relearn even to sit. Also, as muscles do not move for 45 days, they become weak. To regain that flexibility and strength of joints and muscles, one must go for physiotherapy.

There was a tragedy during this physiotherapy at Nanavati Hospital. The person from Nanavati Hospital (a helper to the doctor), during the session of physiotherapy, told me that he would make me cry. I requested him not to harass me, but he went on bending my leg to make me cry. This bending of the leg beyond a limit resulted in a fracture of the right knee joint, so again I had to go through that routine of plaster from toe to armpit for 45 days. Dr. Katrak then advised us that there should not be any force while exercising, and whatever can be achieved by light exercise should be accepted.

Due to this tragic incident, I could not attend school for the entire year of 6th standard. Here again, the arrangement of taking a notebook of one of the students, copying the same at home, and then again handing back that notebook to the student was worked out with the help of the school. At the time of my final exam, the principal raised a technical issue with the minimum attendance required for allowing me to appear for the exam. Pappa met the principal and suggested that he would write a request letter to the education officer to make an exception and allow me to appear for the exam. He requested the principal to write a letter of recommendation to the education officer to consider this request favourably, which she did. Finally, the education officer allowed me to appear for the exam.

Pappa would take me to school, and the school had arranged a place for me on the ground floor where I would write my papers. I appeared for the exam of 6th standard and cleared the same. This arrangement ensured that I did not miss a year.

In the 7th standard, we hired a person who would lift me, travel on the school bus with me, and drop me in the class. The same routine was followed in the evening for coming back home. In the evening, Mummy would take me to a private clinic for physiotherapy. Slowly, I started walking.

From 8th standard, I did not require help and started helping with day-to-day activities at home. One of Pappa's friends, who was in a senior position at IDBI, had come home. Both families would meet frequently, either at his residence (at Cuffe Parade) or at our house. In one of those meetings, Pappa sought his advice about what I should do. He advised that I should join typing classes during the vacation. His logic was that any company, whether big or small, would need a typist, and to become more important in that function, I should learn stenography as well. According to him, this combination would do a lot of good for me, and most importantly it was purely a desk job.

In those days, all correspondence was by typed letters. Big bosses would dictate letters, and typing with stenography would mean that I would be working with top bosses. This advice sounded very logical, so after the SSC exam was over, Pappa asked me when and where I was planning to learn typing. I told Pappa that I respected the advice but that was not what I wanted from life. I also admitted that I had not yet pondered over the question of what I would become if not a typist.

There was a reason for this reply. I always saw myself as a senior person in the company, discussing important matters in the conference room with the senior management. I had not disclosed this to anybody, but I was certain that I would do everything required to achieve this. The only problem was that the destination was clear, but how to reach there was not clear.

Again, one of the better qualities of Pappa was that he never prevailed upon us with his thoughts. Decisions were always based on discussion. So, it was curtains for the subject of becoming a typist. This is not to demean the job of a typist; it is just a question of attempting something higher and dreaming big.

I got first class in the SSCE (scored 62%); this was considered good in those days. I decided to join the commerce stream. Again, the school was very nearby (in those days, 11th standard was in school). This helped me as I could attend the school on my own as it was within walking distance; it was just about a 15-minute walk for me.

For some reason, I lost focus and was just drifting away aimlessly. This could be because, in the earlier school, there were a smaller number of students, and now it was like a mill, with no personal attention from teachers and no real friends as nobody from the previous school joined the new school except for one. This situation perhaps made me uncomfortable, and I lost focus. I cleared the exam of 11th standard, but it was not satisfactory.

Schooling of Maulik

Maulik had finished with all the surgeries; his physiotherapy was still ongoing. On the first day of his schooling at Nanavati School, Mummy was carrying him. One of the teachers of the school saw her; she came and told Mummy that her responsibility ended at the school's gate. From there on, the responsibility was of the school. That teacher lifted Maulik and took him to his class. The surgeries and the physiotherapy worked well for Maulik, and he slowly started walking, first with the help of a walker and then without any support.

Amongst the three of us, Maulik was the brightest and was very bold. He also had a particular attitude towards life right from the beginning.

A few instances from his childhood would reveal his attitude towards life. He stood first in the 1st and 2nd standard; the 2nd rank was of a girl. In the 3rd standard, he stood second, and that girl was 1st. After coming home, Mummy asked him why he stood 2nd. He replied without any feeling of guilt, "This time that girl came 1st."

In one of the oral exams, the teacher asked him, "How many slices are there in the packet of bread?" "14," Maulik replied promptly. The teacher was impressed. In the evening, when he narrated this incident, we were surprised at how he was confident about the number of slices in a pack of bread. "Have you counted them ever, Maulik?" we asked. "No, but the teacher also had not counted!" All of us had a hearty laugh at his presence of mind!

Our grandmother was telling him the story of Ganpati. The incident was how Shankar (Ganpati's father), not knowing that Ganpati was his own son, got angry with him and cut his head. Having realized the mistake, he sent persons to go and bring the head of any living being so that he could implant it on Ganpati's body. People went in search of a living being. When they saw an elephant, they cut its head and handed it over to Shankar. Shankar then implanted the head of the elephant on the body of Ganpati. Maulik did not agree to this solution. He asked, "But Dadi, why did they kill an innocent elephant for the head? Ganpati's own head was lying there. Shankar could have implanted that." My grandmother had never encountered this logic in her life. She was upset and told Maulik that she would never tell him any story. This attitude of Maulik never changed.

Maulik was very mischievous and would continuously argue with our grandparents, but at the same time, he was their pet. When for no reason he stopped walking, our grandmother would offer a special prayer every day, and similarly, when she had undergone surgery for cataract, Maulik would remind her about the eyedrops.

Again, in his case, he had to be shifted to another school as from 5th standard it was becoming a girls' high school. Even though he could have continued for one more year in Nanavati School, it was decided that to avoid any last-minute problems, he should move to Sanskar Jyot in the 4th standard itself.

On the first day of his new school, the teacher asked him about his name, which school he was studying in, and what his rank in the exam was. Maulik replied. She then asked him about the spelling of his name. Maulik could not reply about the spelling as in Nanavati School they did not teach English till 5th standard. The teacher told him that he would have to work hard on this subject.

We had a practice at home; dinner was always together, and everyone would describe events that took place during the day. Maulik narrated the incident of not being able to spell his name in school. From that day onwards, Pappa started teaching English to Maulik. Mummy went to the shop where people sell old papers and books. She bought books on English grammar from there. The result: Maulik stood FIRST in English in the final exam!

Mummy had taught Maulik that it was possible that the other children might not like to play with him, and in that eventuality, BOOK IS THE BEST FRIEND. Maulik took this advice very seriously and developed the habit of reading. In the process, he got the best of both worlds. He used to play with the other children and used to read a lot.

He was quick in grasping, could read extremely fast, inclined languages, could recollect from what he had read, and could use it at the appropriate time. He also had another habit: he would do his homework in the school itself. Because of this habit, after coming home, he could do things he liked. He never had to bother about homework. Another great quality was that he read things only once. Even with that fast reading, he would remember things. He never had to revise.

Going to school for Maulik became problematic as for no known reason he stopped walking. Mummy would carry him from the 2nd floor to catch the school bus. After reaching school, some of his friends would carry him to the class. The same routine was followed for coming back. It was a challenge every day, and during the rainy season, it was more problematic. But Mummy never complained about it, and Maulik never had to ask his friends to carry him. All this was done with lots of smiles and leg-pulling.

Maulik passed the SSC Exam with flying colours.

You may fail but that is a lesser crime as compared to not aiming BIG, taking a path that is very easy can not be the best solution in life, you must aim higher and give your best to achieve the same and you have to accept right at the beginning that the Road to achieve that GOAL is going to be difficult.

Chapter 4

College and Career Path

Shubhani goes to College

Shubhani cleared her SSC exam and decided to join SNDT College to pursue Arts. SNDT college was nearby and this shorter distance again helped. She would go to the college by taxi. Auto rickshaws came much later.

She had a few friends who were staying near our home. They would come home in the morning and would take her to the college in a taxi. In the evening, they would come back in a taxi, drop her at home, and then they would go to their residence.

While she was studying, Pappa was simultaneously working on what she could do after her graduation. He felt that she could be a telephone operator. In those days, since there were no mobile phones, even the smallest organization needed a telephone operator. He spoke to the HR Head of the Company and requested him to permit Shubhani to come for training during her vacations. The HR Head arranged for the training. Shubhani, on her vacation, started getting trained as a telephone operator.

She completed her graduation with English and Economics and was not keen on going for higher studies.

I go to College

I was admitted to Narsee Monjee College of Commerce, which was one of the reputed colleges in Mumbai. For a normal person, the college was just about a 5-minute walk from our residence.

My aimless drifting continued for a few more months; each day was a non-productive day, nothing worth writing home about. This was a difficult period for me as I did not have any real friends in college.

During this period, like in the case of Shubhani, Pappa arranged training for me in the company where he was working. The training was in the Consumer Store of the company. The Consumer Store would purchase grocery items from the market in bulk; since the purchase was in bulk, it would be cheaper. Employees could buy from this Consumer Store and the bill was paid in instalments from their salary.

Pappa thought that after I graduated, this training would allow me to get employment in the company in the Consumer Store. I did not argue; I completed the training, but I knew that this again was not what I wanted from life.

The turning point in my life was one lecture by the principal. There was a tradition in the college; the principal would take one lecture, and all students of First Year Commerce could attend that lecture. In that lecture, apart from other things, the principal advised all the students to appear for the entrance exam of Chartered Accountancy. According to him, this degree would give us an edge over a student who had just a degree of B.Com. This advice gave me the path I was looking for to reach my destination.

I appeared for the CA entrance exam and cracked it. Apart from this degree, I also got very close to other students who, till now, were just acquaintances. For me, now this new path to reach my destination was absolutely clear. I knew what I had to do.

Now graduation was just one milestone, which I completed.

Maulik goes to College

Maulik also joined Narsee Monjee College. Maulik was facing a challenging time at that moment. As he was not able to walk, commutation was a big challenge.

The school friends who had helped Maulik during school days continued with their help. They would come home, lift him to take him down. They would go to college in an autorickshaw and then they would lift him to his class. The same process was followed by his friends for bringing him back home.

The most important aspect of this routine was that this responsibility was shared by a number of friends. They would internally decide who was going to take that responsibility on that particular day.

Only to describe the real effort of those friends, we used to stay on the 2nd floor and his class in the college was on the 3rd floor!

Whenever we went out, Maulik would either stay home or Pappa would carry Maulik. This was, in a way, getting more and more difficult as carrying a person single-handedly was not easy.

To everybody's surprise, like he had stopped walking for no reason, in the same fashion, he stood up one day and started walking. This was really a mystery but it reduced the tension of the entire family to a great extent.

Because of his sense of humour, intelligence, and approach toward life, Maulik was very popular amongst the students and professors. He was so popular that he was the Class Representative (CR) for three continuous years. In the fourth year, he did not stand for the election as one of his very close friends wanted to be CR.

Apart from being excellent in his studies, he was a good writer (he would write poetry and prose in Gujarati and Urdu) and a good orator too. He would participate in the elocution contest. In case there were not enough participants, he would encourage another student to participate. He would tell the other student that he could choose to talk in favour or against the given topic. He would say, "I will take the other side but please participate."

Two of his friends were so close to him that they would sit on the last bench of the class and Maulik would rehearse. They sat on the last bench to correct the throw of Maulik's voice; the pitch of the voice had to be loud enough for everybody to hear but at the same time it should not sound like he was shouting.

Maulik then started representing the college in the elocution contest at Bombay University.

Maulik's friends could be divided into two parts. Friends who had ambitions, had faced a few failures while achieving results but were fighters. The other group was like the top-of-the-world kind. This was the group who had never tasted failure and became big shots in their professional career.

Academically, Maulik belonged to the second group but this superiority did not go to his head and he was equally close with the friends of the first group.

Maulik completed his graduation with flying colours!

One step towards Pappa's and Mummy's efforts to make us self-sufficient. Shubhani gets the Job

Once Shubhani finished her graduation, Pappa informed the Managing Director of the company about her graduation and enquired with him about the possibility of a job for her.

The Managing Director called the HR Head and told him that after three days there was Amavasya and Shubhani would join the company from the next day of Amavasya. Apart from the case of Shubhani, the management of the company, in general, was very sympathetic to physically challenged people.

Obviously, this was a big relief for Pappa and Mummy. Their efforts had given the result for their first child!

Shubhani got the advantage of the training which she had undergone during the vacations of the college. This helped her to perform her duty right from the first day. There was a slight problem, she was the daughter of one of the senior persons of the company and her appointment was in a way approved by the Managing Director. Normally, nobody likes this kind of appointment as it creates a feeling of insecurity and secondly, everybody assumes that everything will be reported to the management. These feelings result in animosity against that person and may result in a kind of non-cooperation. Silent resentment from her colleagues was not unexpected.

All these reasons for insecurity and perceived threats went away slowly as Shubhani was performing her duty like any other employee and never took advantage of the closeness with the top management.

She never took any undue advantage by asking for any favour citing her disability and slowly she started getting popular for performing her duty in a manner that was far better than what was expected from her.

She had a sharp memory for numbers and her ability to remember telephone numbers is phenomenal even today. This strength was a game changer as many senior persons would call her up even on holidays to enquire about the number of a person they wanted to speak to. She never disappointed them.

Another gift was to remember the voice. Once she heard the voice, she would remember that voice, so when that person would call a second time, she would address that person by his/her name. She would also remember the name of the person he/she would ask for, so the person on the other side did not have to tell her anything, she would just confirm with the person. This quality was really appreciated by the person on the other side of the phone. These two qualities helped her to be very quick in her job as every time she did not have to refer to the telephone diary or phone register.

A third plus point was establishing rapport with all the persons who came into her contact, right from the top management to a peon. Not only this, she would also develop rapport with their family members as well.

Due to these qualities, people became fond of her, even when they had not seen her. This appreciation increased further when they saw her in person.

Even today export customers are more important than domestic customers. In those days they were as good as God. They would always get the best of treatment.

When these customers visited the company, they would request the Vice President (Marketing) that they would like to meet the "telephone operator" and after seeing Shubhani performing her duties, they would go back with a lot more appreciation for her.

I decided that I should not be satisfied with simple graduation and opt to go for higher studies

During those days, for a commerce student, there were four alternatives for higher studies: Chartered Accountancy, Company Secretary, Cost Accountancy, or an MBA course. In those days, amongst these four degrees, the ranking of Chartered Accountancy was highest.

To become a Chartered Accountant, one must undergo training under a Chartered Accountant for three years; the term for this training is "Article ship." Company Secretary and Cost Accountancy were correspondence courses. For the MBA course, one had to attend college.

I had passed the CA entrance exam in the second year of B.Com., but I had not started the article ship as that would have been physically too strenuous.

As I had already passed the CA entrance exam, after appearing for the final exam of B.Com., I decided to start my article ship.

In those times, offices of Chartered Accountants in Mumbai were at Fort, VT, Churchgate, or at Marine Lines. We were staying at Vile Parle, a suburb which was about 20 km away from the offices of Chartered Accountants.

When I started the discussion about my decision to go for the course of Chartered Accountancy, it was a big "NO" from everyone. Even my close friends advised me that I should drop the idea as it would be too strenuous for me.

The biggest hurdle which was perceived was how would I go to the office every day. It was not only reaching the office which would be at a far-off place but after reaching the office, I had to work for eight hours and then again come back travelling the distance of 20 km. I had to do this for three years.

In addition to that, one more factor was the monsoon. In the rainy season in Mumbai, there are days when it does not rain, it pours. On days of heavy rains, even a normal person finds it difficult to reach the office as at many places there is waterlogging and commuting becomes challenging.

People advised me that I should go for the course of Company Secretary as it is a correspondence course, so all these difficulties could be avoided.

Mummy was not comfortable at all; she was really perturbed with this idea of mine.

I thought about this problem and came out with a solution. I told her:

- I have travelled by BEST bus for going to college and coming back which was one-stop journey, so there was no issue of getting in and getting out of the bus
- I will take the bus from the first stop while going and coming back, at the first stop people have to stand in a queue, so getting in will not be a problem
- I will get on the bus only if I get a seat

- I will carry one hundred rupees every day with me for any emergency, in case of an emergency I will take a taxi and come home

- I know that the problem of getting tired is not there at all as in school or college one always spends about eight hours, and after coming back from school or college, I have never said that I am tired, so the problem is just our assumption

I sat with Mummy and explained to her all the problems and their solutions and requested her not to oppose this idea. Finally, she agreed, "Alright! If you feel so strongly about it then go ahead." Pappa was also convinced.

I discussed the same points with my close friends, they got convinced which was very important for me. From that day onwards, they were with me like a rock. The first hurdle was crossed.

As per the rules of the Institute of Chartered Accountants of India, there is a limit to the number of article clerks a Chartered Accountant can register under him/her for training.

In those days, an article clerk would get a stipend of Rs. 60 per month in the first year, Rs. 100 in the second year, and Rs. 150 in the third year. An article clerk would work like an employee, so imagine how a Chartered Accountant could let go of this benefit. He / She pays a paltry sum to a student who is, if not brilliant, is at least an above-average student.

Now, for me, it was time to find a Chartered Accountant under whom the article ship can start. The search for the CA firm started. The search turned out to be more difficult than expected. Chartered Accountants who were known to us, directly or indirectly said NO, but that NO was sugar-coated. People who were not known said NO without any hesitation.

One of my professors had his office at Vile Parle, just about ten minutes from our house. If he takes me as an article clerk under him, then all the problems which I had to overcome would simply vanish.

I went to his office, and that professor told me that just about ten days back a particular student of our college had come to meet him and they had signed the papers for the article ship. He said that if that boy cancelled the registration, he would not mind taking me as an article clerk. I even knew that boy but I thought it was not appropriate to request for cancelling the registration.

The search was on but it was not giving any result. But I did not lose my confidence. Even when this search was on, a lot of people were still advising me to drop the idea and go for one of the correspondence courses. I did not pay any attention to this.

There is a very fine line between confidence and overconfidence or between persistence and being adamant, all of which depend upon the result.

One of my uncles was working in the firm of a Chartered Accountant. One of his colleagues had started his own firm and his office was at Fort, opposite Bombay Stock Exchange. My uncle spoke to him, explained the entire situation, and requested him to take me as an article clerk under him. Incidentally, one of my very close friends was an article clerk in the same firm. That person said he would meet me first and would decide about it.

As I had never gone to town on my own, my friend who was working in the same firm suggested that for a few days, he would go with me on the bus and take me to the office.

We reached the office, it was an office where the Boss would sit in the cabin and the staff sat on the mezzanine floor, to reach there one had to climb a steep staircase.

Before we met, he knew that I was physically challenged but when he saw me, he was taken aback. He did not expect my disability to be so severe.

After the initial discussion, he suggested a different route to me, a route which perhaps no article clerk must have taken so far. He told me that we should try this for a week, if we found that I can do it, then we would go ahead with the registration of the article ship. If not, then I should accept that I can't do article ship under him.

I wholeheartedly accepted the suggestion as his apprehension was logical. Despite that, he was giving me a chance, so my article ship had a probation period of seven days.

After this discussion, I went up to the mezzanine floor. As I reached the last but one step of the staircase, I was pleasantly surprised to see the first cousin of my next-door neighbour. Both of us knew each other very well and the relationship was going back many years. This gentleman was a Chartered Accountant and hierarchy-wise was second in command in the firm. He was told that a boy who is physically challenged was going to come to the office for the article ship but he was not told about who was coming. The moment both of us acknowledged each other, I knew that there would be no problem. It was not that I wanted to take advantage of the acquaintance but more like a feeling where you know that ultimately things would fall in place.

In the evening, when I narrated the entire episode, Mummy felt that as the Chartered Accountant could not say no directly, he had taken this indirect route of seven days. I told her that I did not read it like that. According to me, this was really a perfect way of handling the matter. If I was not able to attend office regularly, then I would become a burden on him which I never wanted to be.

On the evening of the fourth day, the boss called me into his cabin and told me that he would call for the registration papers for my article ship. A major hurdle was crossed. In those four days, I also got the confidence that I would be able to travel by the BEST bus on my own, so, I told my friend that I would come to the office on my own from the next day.

The next day I boarded the bus on my own, and got down at the last bus stop (Bombay University), another hurdle was crossed, I looked at the building of Bombay University and made a promise to myself. The promise was "One day I will come over here in my chauffer-driven car."

In those days, there was no relaxation for physically challenged people to get onto the bus from the front door, I had to stand in the queue and wait for the bus which many times used to take a very long time and the bus journey would take a longer time as compared to the train. I requested in the office that I be allowed to leave half an hour early as compared to other article clerks. I was allowed to do so.

In about two months, I got the confidence to travelling and so I, myself, told my boss that I no longer needed that relaxation, I also would leave the office along with other article clerks.

The journey was not a smooth road, there were incidences like on one occasion, I was on the bus and because of rains and gusty wind a tree fell on the road near JJ Hospital, the bus was standing still, it could move ahead only after the tree was removed from the road, by what time that would happen was anybody's guess. There were no mobile phones at that time, a fellow passenger sitting next to me had to get down one stop after JJ Hospital, so he decided that he would walk. I requested him to call up my parents and tell them that I would be late because of this problem and they should not worry. He said he would do that. He called up but the result of that call was completely different than what was expected!

Mummy felt that some people had kidnapped me and by calling them up they were misguiding them so that they would not go to the police station! She panicked and there were heated arguments between her and Pappa. I reached home very late.

When I came to know about what she had thought when she received the call, I jokingly told Mummy, "Why on earth would someone take away the liability from your shoulder onto his shoulder?" Everybody laughed aloud but she laughed with tears rolling down. This is the kind of love that they had for us.

In the office, my friend came to know that the boss thought that I should not be sent for audit work as it was out of Mumbai and there was travelling involved. He told me that he would take care of me if I was sent for audit work.

The next day I went to my boss and told him that I would like to go outstation for the audit work and my friend was ready to take the responsibility. It was then decided that next time when the team would go for audit, I would also go with them. My friend took the entire responsibility and I got the opportunity to do the auditing work. Then of course it became a routine and I went for audit work several times. This gave me confidence that with a bit of help, I could travel also on my own.

One more development that took place during this time was that my friends decided that we should go on a tour to Bangalore, Mysore, Ooty, and Kodaikanal. I was slightly hesitant as I felt that because of me, they perhaps would face problems, particularly when we would go for sightseeing. When I told them, they just brushed aside that apprehension and insisted that I ought to go with them.

Apart from everything else, the one thing that I enjoyed the most was rowing in the lakes of Ooty and Kodaikanal. I had never done rowing earlier and here I was doing it all by myself!

This trip was pathbreaking as this was my first long-distance trip with my friends. Later, there were many including a trip to Kashmir, Kedarnath, Badrinath, Gangotri, and Hemkund Saahib which is situated at 15,000 feet.

Overall, my performance in the CA exams up to a particular point was not bad considering that they were CA exams and so were bound to be tough. But I stumbled on one paper in finals and because of that, took a bit longer time to become a Chartered Accountant.

This was a proud moment for Pappa and Mummy as they had never even imagined that their child would get a professional degree. The three of us always had this advantage. Whatever we did was always considered stupendous. The main reason was that nothing was expected from us. So even for a small achievement, we got a big applause.

Maulik follows suit and also decides to go for higher studies

Maulik was toying with the idea of taking writing as a profession; he was writing prose and poetry while he was in college and they were appreciated by the professors.

One evening, we both discussed in detail whether he should select writing as a profession or go for a post-graduation course. I suggested to him to go for the post-graduation course and gave the logic for my suggestion. He was convinced.

He started pursuing the courses of Chartered Accountancy and Cost Accountancy along with B.Com. The problems related to going to town every day to attend the office were going to be there even for Maulik. The same uncle who had helped me with my article ship came to help Maulik. He told his nephew to take Maulik as an article clerk as his office was very near to our residence.

An interesting episode occurred when he was attending a class on Cost Accountancy. The friend for whom he did not stand for the CR election in the final year of B.Com. was a brilliant student. He was also attending this class. In one of the lectures, the professor asked students about their background. Maulik and his friend told him that they were pursuing Commerce. The professor made a sarcastic comment that this subject was for engineering students and that Maulik and his friend would not be able to clear this paper.

After the lecture was over, Maulik's friend motivated Maulik in his typical friendly manner, "If you fail in this subject then I will kill you!"

Maulik and his friend passed this exam. Once the result was out, his friend came to our house and told Maulik to get ready. Maulik asked him, "Where are we going?" He said, "College."

He took Maulik to college and both went to the staff room to meet that professor. Maulik's friend told him that both of them had passed and told him that he should not pass comments without understanding the calibre of the students.

He was admitted to IIM (Ahmedabad) and rose to the envious position of Vice President of NASCOM. To everyone's shock, he passed away due to cardiac arrest at the age of 41. He had already resigned from NASCOM and wanted to start something where he wanted Maulik to play an important role. Maulik had told him, "Just let me know when and I would be there," but that was not to be.

From the other two very close friends of Maulik, one rose to the position of Group CFO and Executive Director of a listed company and the other one rose to the position of Managing Director of one of the leading fund houses.

Every year Maulik would go to Lonavala with these two friends and their families for a small vacation and all of them during these three days would become college students again.

I am not sure whether it was because of his intelligence, his confidence, his way of handling life, or a combination of all three factors, but Maulik never appeared tense when he was appearing for exams. There was a very big difference in how I appeared for exams and how he appeared. When I appeared, the entire family was tense and in the case of Maulik, everybody was tense except Maulik!

He had a unique style of preparation for the exams. He would sit with all the books which he had to refer to. Against each chapter, he would write the time that he would take to finish that chapter. Adding the time of each chapter, he would know the total number of days he would require to finish the subject. If he would finish that subject earlier than expected, then for the remaining days, he would not study at all. He would take up the next subject as per the timetable that he had fixed and he never had to revise the subject.

There was a tinge of superstition when his results were declared, they were published in the newspaper. It was always I who would see his results and the result was always "Pass." He cleared all his exams on the first attempt.

Maulik obtained two professional degrees; he was a Chartered Accountant and a Cost Accountant. Again, this was a proud moment for Pappa and Mummy (in fact a very proud moment) as their second child had obtained not one but two professional degrees. These qualifications were of their child who underwent surgeries for almost two and a half years, he had to be carried to his school and college but they never gave up hope and always backed him for whatever he wanted to do.

We knew that doing a job was a new phase in our life and that also will have its own challenges, after applying for the job, when you go for the interview and as soon as you enter the room you immediately realise what the decision from other side is going to be. This was in spite of the fact that in my Resume' I used to make it very clear that I am a physically challenged person. In a city like Mumbai, where from suburbs the time taken to reach the office in town is about one and half hour and in 5 minutes you are out from that interview room.

As writer Javed Akhtar puts it "Aadmi chahe kitni bhi himmat rakhale, kabhi kabhi bahot dar lagta hai".

Always remember that there is always a scarcity of people who are HONEST, FULLY DEDICATED to the job, are HARD WORKING and can DELIVER. Demonstrate these FOUR qualities and then the world does not care about your physical deformities

Chapter 5

Professional Careers

I get the Job

When it came to finding a job, people suggested that I should take up the job in the company where Pappa and Shubhani were working. I believed I should get the job on my merits. Even with my qualification as a Chartered Accountant, I was finding it difficult to get a job.

One of the jobs for which I had applied was with a group company of a leading paint manufacturing company. The office was at Nariman Point. I got a call for the interview, and after the interview, the CFO asked me whether I would like to ask any questions. I said that I would just like to clarify about my deformity. I said, "I am aware that I have a deformity but that deformity has not come in the way when it comes to work." I also showed him the letter of the Chartered Accountant under whom I had done my article ship stating that I had worked in his office like any other person.

The CFO promised me that selection would be purely on merits and that deformity would not be the criteria. I thanked him for giving me a level playing field. The second interview was with the directors. This also went off well, and they said they would inform me.

I came home and as we were discussing how the interview went, to our surprise, there was a call from the CFO. He said that the directors wanted to meet my father and it would be better if that meeting could take place the next day. I checked with Pappa about his availability and he agreed.

The next day, Pappa and I went to Nariman Point for the meeting. The CFO requested me to wait at the reception and took Pappa to meet the directors. They had one apprehension, "Whether I will be able to get along with the people and work as a team?" Pappa assured them that this had never been a problem, be it school, college, or even during the article ship and they should not worry about it at all.

I was then called inside and all of them congratulated me and wished me a successful career. My first job started on 4th July 1986. It was Maulik's birthday. Office timings were 9:30 a.m. to 5:30 p.m. I found out about the contract bus which was reaching Nariman Point by 9:00 a.m., and in the evening would start from Nariman Point at 10 minutes to 6:00 p.m. This was a suitable timing except for the fact that in the evening from my office building to the spot from where the contract bus was leaving was a 20-minute walk for me. Coming down from the 7th floor in the lift and then a 20-minute walk was making it too tight as the bus would start exactly at 10 to 6, it would not wait.

I requested the CFO to allow me to go five minutes earlier than the office timings. The CFO agreed without any hesitation and the problem of commuting from Ville Parle to Nariman Point and back was solved.

Very soon, I could develop a rapport with my colleagues and seniors. My nature and sense of humour perhaps played a major role in this, and I was accepted wholeheartedly by everyone in the office.

In the office, there was only one computer. This computer was used only to prepare the sales invoice and it had a database of customers. I wanted to learn computers for doing work in the office. I was reaching the office by 9:00 a.m., the other staff would reach by 9:30 a.m., and they would take about 15 to 20 minutes to freshen up. So, I had about 45 minutes in the morning which I could utilize for learning.

I again went to the CFO and asked for permission to learn on that computer in these 45 minutes. The CFO agreed to it but with the condition that the key of "Delete" should never be used.

I started learning "Lotus 123" and "WordStar". After a few days of learning, I realized that I could use "Lotus 123" for submitting documents to the bank which would improve the accuracy of the statement and would also reduce the time of preparation of the statement. I started using "WordStar" for writing official letters. Seeing this, the company decided that it would go for one more computer which would be exclusively used by me.

Our factory was in Gujarat and I had to visit the factory once in three months. My rapport with the CFO was extremely good. After about four years, I felt that my career was not shaping up. I had a frank discussion with him and expressed my pain area. He explained to me that if the company did not grow then our own growth also was difficult.

During this time, the CFO of the company where Pappa and Shubhani were working once told Pappa, "I need a Chartered Accountant, I agreed with the feeling of Shakti when he was looking for a job after passing. Now the scenario is different, we need a Chartered Accountant and if the vacancy can be filled by a known person, why should I look for a person outside?"

I was offered the job in the Accounts department with an additional responsibility of MIS. I resigned from the company where I was working and the best part was that all formalities were completed without any cribbing. It was a very peaceful parting. On a few occasions, they called me to explain things to the new person and I went there and did that part with no grudges. In fact, it was always a pleasure meeting them.

Over here also after about four years, I started feeling that my career was stranded. The CFO of the earlier company and I were in regular touch. He had joined another group company of the same leading paint manufacturing company. Once he called me and told me that he was looking for a Chartered Accountant who could look after the finance function. I always wanted to work in the finance department, so accepted his offer.

I managed to achieve what was expected from me but somewhere down the line there were issues with the CEO and I left that organization and went back to the same company from where I had come.

I got a real opportunity when the company went for a demerger. The CFO, seeing my potential, gave me the responsibility of accounts and finance-related issues that arise upon demerger. I successfully completed that task. The senior management of the company earlier had an apprehension about how a person like me who had physical deformities and was very short in height would be able to discuss the subject of finance with the banks and financial institutions.

My performance in the entire episode of Demerger cleared the doubt in the mind of management. My role was enhanced, instead of only accounts now I was to handle finance as well. My dream of going to the office in my car and attending meetings with the senior management of the company was fulfilled.

One dream was still pending, the dream of going abroad for official work. Then, going abroad was still a big thing.

The demerger of the company created one more opportunity for me. The CFO gave me the responsibility of handling the accounts and finances of the subsidiary company in Antwerp (Belgium). When the MD and the Finance Director came to know about this development, they called the CFO for a discussion. In that meeting, they told him that definitely, I was doing more than what was expected but sending me abroad was out of the question.

They were apprehensive on account of three things - long flight hours and who would help me in Antwerp if needed. Also, they were not sure whether the Europeans would be comfortable dealing with a person with a deformity and short height. The apprehension was more out of real concern for me. After this meeting was over, the Finance Director called me and told me in no uncertain terms that I would not be sent to Antwerp and I should not feel bad about it.

I immediately responded that for me the work was more important. The MD and Finance Director thought that the matter had been addressed and put to rest. But the CFO thought I would be able to do my job far better if I went to Antwerp and met the concerned persons personally. After a few months of my handling of the subject, I developed a good rapport with the employee who was stationed at Antwerp. The CFO talked to that person and told him that he intended to send me to Antwerp and asked him whether he would take care of me. He was assured that there would not be any problem and I should visit Antwerp. There was one more comfort, a very big comfort, my very good friend was also at Antwerp.

After I got my visa and tickets, the MD and Finance Director once again discussed the matter with the CFO and checked about all arrangements. The CFO told them that he was confident that there would be no problem.

On the previous day before flying, I told everybody at home and my friend about my visit. Mummy was upset with me for not informing her earlier. I explained to her the reason behind not discussing it earlier. I said that if for some reason they did not send me to Antwerp, then everybody at home would be disappointed. If it is not discussed, then only I would be disappointed.

The trip to Antwerp was very successful not only from the work point of view but also in boosting my confidence. My second dream was also realised.

This trip also gave confidence to the MD and the Director Finance and then I went to Belgium several times.

To say that my colleague and his wife and my friend and his wife took very good care of me is really an understatement. The hospitality in all those visits that I received from them can only be experienced, it can never be described in words.

They took me to some of the beautiful places in Belgium and other countries like France, Germany, Amsterdam, and Luxembourg.

I was climbing the ladder in the organisation and more importantly, I was always chosen as a core team member whenever something new and challenging in the company took place. In 2016, the promoters of the company decided to sell their stake to a Japanese multinational company and I was designated as Vice President (Finance and Accounts). That company used to hold a global meeting of the Accounts and Finance persons every two years. I got an opportunity to go to Japan to attend that meeting. After completing the work, I went sightseeing in Tokyo and Kyoto. The most important thing was that on the trip to Kyoto, I was alone.

In January 2019, I had a fall and had a fracture of my femur bone. I had to undergo surgery for the same. As our bones are brittle right from our birth, recovery takes a longer time. My company took very good care of me by arranging my stay after the surgery at the guesthouse of the company which was near our office. I had to sleep straight for four and a half months. Forget about getting up, I was not even allowed to turn sides. Staying at the guesthouse really helped as my colleagues would come to discuss matters. I also started attending conferences through video calls and started doing my work on the laptop, all this was in the sleeping position. Still, there were days when I would feel low. Shubhani would then tell me about the surgery which she also had to undergo when her wheelchair got overturned in the office and she had fractured her femur bone. She told me, "You are lucky. So many people come and meet you. You are doing your work for most of the day and can watch TV. I had killed my time by counting crows and pigeons I saw during the day. I could not go to the office for three months but finally, I did resume."

After four and a half months of bed rest, my physiotherapy started and slowly, I started walking again. After seven months, I resumed my office by walking with the help of a walker.

Theoretically, I was to retire in November 2020 but the company asked me to continue. After completing the extended period of two years, in November 2022, I decided to hang my boots.

Dreaming is not a one-time activity. As I started climbing up in the organisation, I wanted to reach a particular position, which I could not. This still pains me sometimes.

Maulik takes up the work

A brother of one of the directors of the company where I was working was looking for a Chartered Accountant. I approached him with the resume of Maulik. He called Maulik and after a discussion, he appointed Maulik as a consultant in his company. His office was in town and Maulik joined the same contract bus in which I was travelling.

After the completion of two years, an opportunity arose in one of the group companies of the company where Pappa, Shubhani, and myself were working. The company was at Vadodara. Maulik appeared for the interview and got the job.

It was a very difficult decision as he was going to stay alone in Vadodara. But as usual, challenges could never put pressure on us. In 1989, he shifted to Vadodara. While taking up the job he was very clear that this would be only for five years after which he wanted to start something on his own. He established himself in this company and was always consulted by the top management not only for subjects related to finance, accounts, or costing but also in many other important matters. Because of this, he really got exposure in several fields.

Maulik had off on the 2nd and 4th Saturdays. He was so attached to the family that on Friday night he would take a train and come to Mumbai and would take the train on Sunday night for Vadodara. This routine never changed. He would have no luggage; only a book which he would finish on the train journey. On other Sundays, he would go to stay at our uncle's house.

His liking towards reading was so strong that on one occasion a person who was in the same compartment asked something to Maulik. Maulik was reading the book, he looked at the person, answered, and started reading the book again. The passenger tried again by asking a second question, and the result was the same, so the fellow passenger asked him, "Are you going to do this the entire journey?" Maulik laughed and closed the book.

In the initial period, he was staying in the company's guest house but later he and one of his colleagues took a flat on rent.

Having settled in the career whereby now one has a steady stream of remuneration, the next immediate stage in the life of everybody is marriage, which is normally referred as "settling in life".

Chapter 6

Personal Lives and Relationships

Marriage

Maulik was very clear; he did not want to marry. Shubhani also was thinking along the same lines, but when two proposals came from friends of Pappa, she went to see those boys. She was greatly disappointed and rejected both of them. She then requested Pappa and Mummy not to pursue that subject and the matter was settled.

I had a different view on the subject. I thought that I would marry if the girl did not have any disability. My logic was, that if I married a girl with a disability, then I was adding one more problem for Pappa and Mummy. But if that girl did not have any disability, then she could be of help to our family. Secondly and most importantly, as a family, we were to give that girl a much better life than many girls could think of.

Once, when I came back from the engagement ceremony of my friend (who was the first one to get engaged), Mummy asked me a very important question. She said, "Now all your friends will start getting married and they with their wives will have their own group, what will happen to you then?" I was not prepared for this question, but my reply was instant. "If they continue to keep me in the group as they have been so far then nothing like it, otherwise, I can't pile myself up on them."

I tried very hard to find an appropriate girl for myself (all possible ways were tried), but did not meet anybody who was worth considering. Then came a proposal from one of the relatives; the girl was staying in one of the cities of Gujarat.

Pappa and I went to see that girl. The meeting was cordial and the response from their side also looked very positive. We parted with the understanding that the next day, I and that girl would meet somewhere outside to understand each other better and then we would decide. While we were leaving their house, her parents asked me, "Will you talk to your mother today and inform her?" I said, "No, I will inform her once we finalise."

To our surprise, the next day they called up early in the morning and said that they would not like to go ahead with the proposal. Pappa was, of course, disappointed but was trying to cheer me up. I was upset not because the proposal did not work out, but because I thought it was I who was going to decide, and instead, it was they who decided. After thinking over their reply, I told Pappa that "I am more surprised rather than disappointed as I am not able to get the reason for them to reject me".

While coming back, at the airport, both of us decided that we would tell Mummy that apart from having a short height that girl had no other problem. It was a mistake, and we should have gone only after proper enquiry.

Despite the best of my efforts, I could not find the match and I wanted to marry only if I met the girl who was fitting into my scheme of things. I decided that I was done with the subject.

To my surprise, that girl from Gujarat, along with her friend, came home after 21 years to meet me. She said it was not her parents but their relative, a very senior person, who told them not to go ahead with the proposal, and they could not say no to him. She and her family were ready for the marriage now. I told her that I had grown beyond that and now I did not want to get into that subject. Today we are friends, and she comes home to meet me and spends time with me for a few days.

Answer to Mummy's Question of What If I Am Not Married

Mummy's apprehension of me getting isolated on account of my friends getting married and me remaining unmarried turned out to be absolutely wrong. Today the situation is that not only my friends are my friends but even their wives are my friends. Many a time, in a tricky situation, I talk to their wives first and then take a decision. They always take me along with them for outstation trips and take so much care that it is difficult to describe.

There is one more layer to it. In addition to their wives, their children are also my friends, and on several occasions, when only the children meet for dinner, they invite me and we all have a lot of fun. I find this really gratifying.

The same is the case with our neighbours in Mumbai, who helped me when I was alone in Mumbai for 30 years. Without their help, it simply would not have been possible. This closeness with the neighbours of Mumbai is because of the good times that we all had right from our childhood. We used to play almost all the games and the competitiveness was fierce. No concessions were given to us and they never played with an attitude that they were obliging us. At that time, all of us were equal.

The bond is so strong that even today they visit us at Vadodara from Mumbai and that trip is only to meet us.

Honestly, I have never felt LONELY like everybody tells you that you would feel if you are not married. In my opinion it all depends upon the kind of other interests that you have in life which determines whether you feel lonely or not.

I don't think even Maulik or Shubhani also ever felt LONELY.

Chapter 7

Decision to Shift to Vadodara

As a family, the thought of whether Mumbai was the right place for us or not was getting discussed now more frequently and with more seriousness. The most important reason was the quality of life in Mumbai.

Secondly, we also knew that with ageing, the ability of Pappa and Mummy to help us would reduce whereas our requirement for help would increase. Quality and the cost of a helper could be a problem as Mumbai is more commercial.

As an alternative, Vadodara looked like a better place for shifting. Maulik's decision to take up the job in Vadodara in 1989 was in a way the first step towards that plan.

Pappa was to retire in October 1993. One of the group companies of the company where he was working was putting up a plant near Vadodara and they offered Pappa to take up that responsibility.

Now the question was the job for Shubhani and myself. Shubhani was highly respected in the group for her efficiency at work and I was professionally qualified, so they assured Pappa that both of us would be placed appropriately in their group companies at Vadodara.

But I decided to stay back in Mumbai because of better prospects and secondly, we as a family wanted to keep a flat in Mumbai for any eventuality.

In November 1993, Pappa, Mummy, and Shubhani shifted to Vadodara. Everybody had thought that with my limitations, I would not be able to stay alone and would also shift soon. Pappa was an exception! He handed over a letter to me at the railway station in which he said, "I am very confident that you will not only be able to stay alone but I know that you will continue to be as systematic in your stay as you always have been."

Another example of how he could motivate and bring the best out of us!

As promised, Shubhani was offered a job in one of the group companies at Vadodara. She joined that company immediately upon reaching Vadodara and Pappa took up the job at the new company.

When the family was finally shifting to Vadodara, the kind of farewell Shubhani got from everybody, starting from workers to officers to executives to managers to senior persons of the company to the directors who, with their family members, would come to meet Shubhani to wish her for her new assignment. A classic example is that we were invited for dinner by the mother and the wife of the Vice President (Marketing). They had so much love and affection for Shubhani.

After working with the company for fourteen years with exemplary performance, the farewell was like a dream.

Maulik starts his Consultancy firm

After five years, Maulik, as per his original plan, announced to the family that he intends to start on his own. This meant that Maulik would again start from ZERO and would have to struggle again. Mummy was not happy and wanted Maulik to drop this idea as he had already established himself in the company.

She called me up and explained to me why she was not in favour of that idea. I went to Vadodara specifically to discuss this matter and convinced her that she should not discourage Maulik and should allow him to go ahead with this decision. I explained to her that we should give Maulik at least three years to establish himself and we would not discourage him during those three years even if he did not earn a single Rupee. Our understanding was very clear **"Maulik will never compromise"**; we were all there for him.

I also assured her that Maulik always achieved what he wanted and this decision would not be an exception. Pappa was always confident about the decisions taken by three of us, Mummy also then agreed, my visit to Vadodara was successful.

During the period of his job, Maulik had met one of the industrialists. Maulik would discuss with him about several issues and he was impressed with Maulik. During one of these meetings, he came to know that Maulik planned to start a company. The main objective of the company would be to advise Medium and Small Companies to grow. When he came to know about this, he told Maulik, "Whenever you decide to start the consultancy firm, please let me know, I will be your first client."

Today, we may not understand the real value of this statement, but it meant a lot to us. Somebody was ready to back Maulik. Maulik then put in his papers. The company was reluctant to let him go. Maulik explained to them the reason. Eventually, they did accept his resignation but it took a long time to relieve him from his responsibilities.

Maulik on a particular day went to the office and announced to all the concerned persons that it was his last day in the office. He would not mind staying back for more hours on that day, but he was not to come from the next day. They finally agreed for parting.

To have some regular income, Maulik tied up with a management institute in Vadodara and started teaching. Students really liked and respected him for his way of teaching and his teachings on other subjects of life. Every year many of them would come home to wish him and take his blessings.

When Maulik handed over the first cheque which he had earned as a professional fee to Mummy, she could not control her tears. She told him about the request that she had made to the doctor on the day he was born. The request of "please kill him." Maulik comforted her with a smile. This smile was a very typical smile, he gave that smile when he wanted to convey that he was aware of what had happened but he had not taken it to his heart.

He also started a magazine called "IT SO HAPPENED" which was published every fortnight and covered important events that occurred in the world in those fifteen days and his own interpretation of these events (this was the era where there was neither Internet nor the 24 hours news channels). This was real hard work and it was subscription-based. This helped him to remain in touch with his would-be clients, the very important industrialists of Vadodara.

After the announcement of the Union Budget, he would be invited by professional circles to give his views on the Budget, he would analyse the budget and explain the macro picture.

During the five years of his job, on one occasion he met the Dean of the Management Studies of Vadodara University. He saw potential in Maulik and both clicked as a team. He was in a way a mentor to Maulik. He took Maulik to the USA several times for professional assignments. These assignments were from a person of Indian origin who had transformed telecommunications in India. He was so impressed with Maulik that he would take up each project only after Maulik gave the green signal.

Maulik's friend flew this aircraft for sightseeing. Maulik at the client's office in the US.

Unfortunately, the mentor was diagnosed with cancer and despite getting the best treatment from doctors in the USA, he passed away at a very young age. This was a very big blow to Maulik as this was the second person who apart from being a mentor, was so intelligent, was a close friend and who he lost.

Professionally Maulik started doing very well and the main contributor was word of mouth by his clients. One of his assignments was with a paint manufacturing company, the promoter of this company was Indian but had settled in the USA. A point came when he suggested to Maulik that he was handing over his cap of CEO to Maulik. Maulik was given full authority to run the company including handling banking transactions. Handing over the handling of bank accounts to a third person speaks a lot about the faith that he had in Maulik.

Maulik would spend half a day in that company and in the second half he would go to his own office. He successfully handled the operations of the company and handed over the reins to that gentleman when he came back from the US. He insisted that Maulik had to continue his association with the company as a director.

His reputation in Vadodara as a professional was growing rapidly and he reached the position of Chairman of the Central Gujarat Zonal Council of the Confederation of Indian Industry (CII) – the most prestigious Industry association of India.

Truly like a very famous ghazal of Mirza Ghalib "Hazaaron Khwahishen Aisi ke har Khwahish pe Dam Nikle" Maulik was fond of many things. One such thing was Urdu Nazms and Ghazals, in fact, he himself wrote nazms.

One such nazm which he wrote on his fiftieth birthday was…

*अबलापा था मैं

जब राह पे लाया गया मुझको

ना आरज़ू सफ़र की

ना चाहत मंज़िल की

ना रोशनी की किरन कोई

ना साथ रेहबर कोई

कदम- ब – कदम बढता गया

कुछ इस तरह कि मेरा नक्शे पा

आज जब देखता हूँ तो सोचता हूँ

कि कहाँ से शुरुआत की थी

कहाँ तक पहुँचा हूँ आज

ऐ ज़िंदगी तेरा शुक्रिया कि शायद तूने

अपने कंधो पे बिठा लिया मुझको

वरना खुद यह सफर तय किया हो मैंने

यह तो मुमकिन न था

ऐ ज़िंदगी तेरा शुक्रिया

उन तमाम बातों के लिये,

उन तमाम रातों के लिये,

जो जाग जागकर काटी मैंने;

उन तमाम नींदों के लिये,

जिनके कंधों ने उठा ली मेरी सारी परेशानियाँ;

उन तमाम ख्वाबों के लिये,

जो मैंने देखे भी नहीं थे और तूने पूरे कर दिए;

उन तमाम दोस्तों के लिये,

जिनका हाथ पकडकर इतनी दूर तक आ पाया मैं,

उन तमाम लोगों के लिये,

जिन्होंने होसले का दीया हरदम जलाये रखा

मैं किस किसका शुक्रगुज़ार हूँ

अब क्या बताउँ तुझसे,

इक तिनका जब हवाओं के सर चढकर

सूरज से रु-ब-रु होता है

तब वह किसका शुक्रिया अदा करे?

बस गर्दन झुकाए

खुदको यह याद दिलाए

कि यह तेरी हैसियत न थी,

हवाओं की ज़र्रा नवाज़ी थी!

[*Meaning: I was a person with disabilities when I had started my journey, I had no desire, no ambition as the path was dark and I was all alone. No one was there to accompany me in my endeavour. Still, I continued walking on my path step by step and now while looking back at my path, I realise I have covered a very long distance! My dear Life! I am grateful to you for lifting me on your shoulders and bringing me till here as it was almost impossible for me to travel such a long journey on my own. I am grateful to you for all those trivial issues and sleepless nights when I could not sleep. I am grateful for the sound sleep that you offered me and I could rest forgetting all my problems. I am grateful for those dreams that I had never woven but are fulfilled today. I am also grateful for all those friends my life gifted me, as they always supported me. I am grateful to all those who always encouraged me. My life has provided me with so many angels, whom to mention and whom to ignore? If a small piece of straw goes up with the wind and finds itself in front of the Sun, straw needs to remind itself that it is not its achievement. It was possible because of the help of the wind.]*

If Shubhani and I could write like Maulik, even we would have written the same.

Another such thing which he could discuss was the art of making a film or a drama. One of his professional assignments was with a film director, and during the discussion, he realised that Maulik, apart from finance and accounts, could also discuss a lot of things about movie making.

At that point of time, he was working on a script for a film and seeing Maulik's interest, he started discussing the script of the film with him. The movie was released and the name of the film was "Road, Movie". In the titles of the film, he gave credit to Maulik as Associate Producer.

Maulik's childhood interest in solving quizzes continued. There was one corporate quiz show named "Brand Equity." Competing in the same was a big thing at that time, and the progress of the competing teams from the regional level to the national level was reported in the Economic Times. It was compered by Derek O'Brien (now the spokesperson of the political party TMC). Maulik and his two colleagues who were working in the company at Vadodara participated in that quiz. Only to convey their real brilliance, none of them made any extra effort in preparation for participating in the regional round; all three were working till the last moment before they left for the quiz.

They won the regional competition and moved on to the national level. In nationals, they won the bronze medal and a return ticket to Dubai. The level of preparation for nationals was the same as it was with the regional round.

Maulik recollected that event in March '23. He wrote:

"This day 26 years ago. What a memory!

I, along with my two colleagues, participated in the Ahmedabad round of the Brand Equity Quiz. The quiz master was the inimitable Derek O'Brien.

After 4 rounds, we were in 7th position (out of 8 teams) and the only thing we thought we could fight for, was not to finish at the bottom of the list!

But then the tide turned and how! Last round, last question, 10 points on offer. If we got that right, we would be the winners. If not, we would finish 3rd.

Lo and behold! The simplest question was lobbed in our direction. 'What was coffee called in ancient China'? We got it right and broke the monopoly of the team that had been winning for the past three years!

Cannot forget the evening!

The crowd was on its feet for this unbelievable turnaround in the fortunes and one gentleman who was recording it on camera took the trouble of finding our address and mailing the video tape to us! Thank you, sir!

I am told that for several years after the event, Derek would mention this turnaround to teams that were struggling that it can still be done.

It certainly can! ☺ ”

Maulik then started quiz show in Vadodara and continued it for several years. He would select the questions and he would be the quiz master.

“Vadodara” Opens a New Chapter in Our Life

Mummy always wished for “apana khud ka ghar.” As usual, Maulik took the initiative and found a good flat. It was a new building, and after taking advice from my uncle, Maulik paid token money for the same. The flat is in the best locality of Vadodara.

Maulik and his colleague, who was also a very good friend, had taken a flat on rent. The friend started looking for an alternative arrangement when he came to know that Maulik's family was coming to Vadodara. When Maulik came to know about this, he told his friend that if you are not comfortable with the situation then there is no force, but we as a family have no problem if you stay with us. Maulik's friend said then he would not look for another place.

When we moved into the new flat, Mummy was extremely happy as her very long pending wish got fulfilled. Maulik's friend also moved in and stayed with us. Today, he, his wife, and two daughters are like family.

There was a similar instance, when Maulik and his two colleagues won the prize of tickets for Dubai (in Brand Equity), they were invited by one of Maulik's friends at Muscat. She and her husband took very good care of them. After a few years, unfortunately, the friend had a severe attack of asthma and passed away. By then, her husband had also become a friend of Maulik. He had shifted to Canada, he came to Vadodara for a professional assignment. He also stayed with us till he completed his assignment.

Along with one of his trips to the USA, Maulik went to Canada. His friend and his second wife took very good care of him and they took Maulik to see some of the beautiful places in Canada.

Before Pappa, Mummy, and Shubhani shifted to Vadodara, Maulik and his friend, who were sharing the flat, were not happy with the tiffin service and on many occasions, they just could not eat anything from the tiffin. They had to go with bread and coffee.

Just before shifting, Pappa was at Vadodara and through somebody came across Sangita. She had recently got married. Pappa requested her to prepare food for Maulik and his friend. This arrangement was only for three months as Pappa, Mummy, and Shubhani were to shift to Vadodara by then. When they shifted to Vadodara, Sangita thought that perhaps now they would not require her services. But she was asked to continue. Pappa then met her husband (Jayendra) and taught him driving. Once he got the license, Pappa kept him as a driver.

After a few years, Jayendra and Sangita had a baby boy (Jay). Jay used to come home with Sangita almost every day. Pappa had a unique ability; he could become a child with a child, a teenager with a teenager, and an adult with an adult, and all of them would enjoy the company of Pappa.

A bonding started taking place between Jay and Pappa. Mummy also liked Jay. Now the situation was that Jay started getting the attention and love of a grandson. He used to address Pappa as Dada, Mummy as Baa, Shubhani as Didi, and Maulik and me as Maulik kaka and Shakti kaka.

Every day Jay would come with Sangita to Dada's house. Grandson and Grandfather both would wait for each other. The most important thing is that it was not only about addressing; Jay, Sangita, and Jayendra really considered Pappa as Jay's Dada and Mummy as Baa.

Pappa started bringing up Jay the way he had brought us up. He would play games with Jay (almost every day), would take Jay along with him when he would go out for some work, would take him out for a drive. Along with these things, he would also teach him like he taught us. Apart from the other teachings, two important things were, how to respectfully talk to elder people and table manners.

One of the most important qualities of Pappa was that he never gave lectures, it was always by real example. For example, when it came to handwriting, he would sit beside you when you were doing homework. Then he would teach you how much space one should keep between two words, how you should write in a straight line. In the "WORD" of "MS Office," we have a function called "Justified" (Control + J). If you refer to any of his diaries or any letter written by him, you will know what is "Justified" and the writing would be absolutely clean.

How did he inculcate the habit of saving? He opened a bank account for Jay like he had done for us when we were young. Then every month he would take Jay with him to sell old papers. From there they would directly go to the bank, he would give the slip book to Jay for filling it up and that amount would be deposited in Jay's account.

When he would be driving, Jay would sit next to him. He would explain to Jay about the role of the gear and taught him about how to change gears. Then he would press the clutch and tell Jay to change the gear. Jay at that young age knew how to change gears.

Pappa was a good swimmer; he decided to teach swimming to Jay, so he took a membership for him and Jay in a club, and every day both of them would go for swimming. For many years they went for swimming.

The bonding of Jay with the entire family was so strong that once Sangita prepared a good dish and for some reason, Jay had not come with her. Jay knew about what was cooked, so he asked Sangita to give that item to him when they were having their dinner. To tease him, Sangita told him that she had not brought anything from Dada's house as they had not given anything to her. Jay said confidently, "That is impossible, they would not eat without giving it to me!" Sangita and Jayendra were amused by that confidence of Jay. She got up and gave Jay what she had brought.

This relationship between Jay and Pappa was known to almost everyone. When Pappa visited his friends or our relatives, he would take Jay with him and Jayendra and Sangita's relatives would invite Pappa to all their functions. The height came when they performed the thread ceremony of Jay. Certain rituals had to be performed by the grandfather of Jay. Jay's real grandfather called up Pappa and told him, "You are his grandfather, please perform the rituals and please do not misunderstand me, I am not offended at all." Pappa performed the rituals.

Jay finished his education and graduated in Mechanical Engineering.

Pappa Retires and is ready to Re-Tire himself

Pappa worked till he was 65 and then decided to call it a day. This retirement was only from work of the office, in his farewell speech he said I am ready to Re-Tire myself and he was true to his words.

Shubhani worked with the company from 1993 to 2020, i.e. 27 years. After completing a total service period of 41 years (including the period of extension of one year after the due date of her retirement and 14 years of service in Mumbai), she decided that it was time. She also called it a day.

Perhaps it was because of tiredness on account of fighting every day for so many years or it was due to good and comfortable times which were not even dreamt of, that created a kind of fear in Mummy's mind that somebody would harm us. It was a case of depression. Slowly the sickness aggravated. With medication, doctors could suppress it but they could never cure it.

Now for Pappa, it was a twin responsibility, taking care of us and Mummy. He without complaining even for a day took up this challenge also. Age was now affecting Mummy, she was finding it difficult to walk. One day she fell and fractured her thigh bone. She had to be operated on.

Upon surgery, she developed certain complications and was shifted to ICU. Pappa would go to the hospital in the morning and Jayendra at night.

She could not recover and on 1ˢᵗ October 2010, she breathed her last.

In the crematorium, one of Maulik's friends, who was also very close to Pappa, asked him, "Uncle, from tomorrow, how is it going to be without Aunty?" Pappa replied, "Many years back, I have had a word with GOD, I have told him, you are free to put me into any condition, I will always LIVE HAPPILY."

Pappa's most favourite song was, "Mere hathile Shyam, Main bhi hath pe adaa hun, thokar laga de, Main tere raste me pada hun" sung by Pankaj Malik. This song is not from any film. The other song was "Karun kya Aas Niraas bhayi" sung by Kundanlal Saigal from the film "Dushman."

If you have not heard, then you should hear both the songs, they are worth listening to. Apart from the benefit of lifting your morale (when you are down), it will also tell you the fundamentals which Pappa had adopted.

Pappa adjusted to the new reality from day one. His routine of exercise and walking continued. He was very clear; he wanted to be physically fit as he had to take care of us. He wanted to help us as long as possible.

At the age of 85, he decided to learn painting. He was inspired by the Managing Director of the company where he was working. This was another principle which Pappa followed. **"If somebody can do a thing, then even I can do it."**

The teacher would come twice a week to teach him painting with crayon. He was surprised by the speed of his progress. In just 18 months, he had completed more than 100 paintings. They were so good that people advised him to go for an exhibition. Maulik's friends helped Pappa in organising the exhibition and it was a huge success.

Chapter 8

A Great LOSS...

At the time of COVID, everybody at home followed strict precautions to avoid catching COVID. As Pappa was 86 and Maulik had asthma, for both of them COVID could create a big problem. Jay shifted to Dada's house so that Pappa would not have to go out for buying things and to help us in any other matter that may arise during COVID times. Earlier to this, many times he would stay at Dada's house as he felt very secure and relieved sleeping next to Dada. But this time it was to help Dada; he stayed for almost two years.

Jay got engaged to Nandini, who is a computer engineer, and the marriage was fixed on 10th February 2022. They decided to go ahead with the marriage as by that time COVID had almost gone and people were moving freely. The marriage was at the native place of Jayendra, which is about a 3-hour drive from Vadodara. We at Vadodara had still not given up on the precautions that were followed during the lockdown.

Despite these precautions, Pappa caught COVID in the last week of January '22. Pappa was never seen to be so anxious about attending any marriage, but he was very concerned as he wanted to attend Jay's marriage. Even Jay was very concerned as he wanted Dada to be present when he was getting married. Pappa had quarantined himself in his room and would open the door only to fetch food and water.

Pappa got cured before the marriage and he consulted doctors about attending the marriage. Everyone wanted to be very sure as attending the marriage would mean six hours of driving in a day and the tiredness from attending the function. The doctors gave him the green signal as he had got cured completely.

Pappa, Shubhani, and Maulik went to attend the marriage, and both the families (of Jay and Nandini) including their relatives were very happy to receive them. Nandini and her family also have a very high regard for all of us.

After coming back from there, Pappa again started having bouts of fever; he had to be hospitalised. This hospitalisation was meant only to ensure that he gets the proper treatment and doctors were expecting discharge in about three days. But the situation started getting difficult for him and he was shifted to ICU. I went to Vadodara when I came to know about Pappa being in ICU. In the morning Jayendra would take me to the hospital and I would sit with Pappa. At night, Jayendra would go and sleep there. Jayendra had taken up this responsibility even when Mummy was in ICU.

Pappa was never in favour of extending life with the help of medical apparatus; he was not happy at all when he was shifted to ICU. I went to the hospital along with Jay and we both requested him to give us a time of three days. We said, "If you don't improve by then, then we will not push you." He looked at both of us and like a king said, "Jao Diye." He had not lost that sense of humour even in those conditions.

Pappa fought hard and was almost at the finish line of recovery. On 10th March, the physiotherapist came to show the exercises that he should do at home. He told her that this was something which he did every day. After she left, he told me, "Abhi usne dekha hi kya hai."

He was to be discharged on 11th March 2022. But on 10th night, again he had a very high fever and all parameters went for a toss. I called up the doctor to understand the status, and the doctor told me that we brought him from zero to a condition where he could go home, but at that moment they were again at zero and things now might not improve.

Shubhani, Maulik, and I discussed the course of action. Shubhani told me, "We THREE know very well that we will be the worst sufferers but Shakti, now we should allow him to GO. If they suggest a ventilator then tell them - NO." Maulik and I agreed with what she was suggesting, of course with a very heavy heart.

I went to the hospital and the lady doctor, as expected, asked me whether we should put him on a ventilator. I said no. To make sure, she asked me, "Don't you want to consult any of your relatives?" I said, "I have come here after discussing this point." She gave me a paper which I had to sign, a formal refusal to put a patient on a ventilator. I signed it. Her first reaction was, "You have done a good thing, even with a ventilator he will not make it." In about 15 minutes, she came back to call me. She said, "Please come inside. He is leaving."

When I reached there, Pappa was unconscious. I asked the doctor if I could tell him something. Will he be able to hear? The doctor said, "We do not know but you can try." I could manage only to say, "Pappa don't worry about us."

I wanted to tell him so many things. Most importantly, I wanted to tell him that we were "really sorry" for disturbing his and Mummy's life completely and wanted to "thank big" to both of them for putting so much effort tirelessly, year after year in preparing three of us to lead a very fulfilling life and while leaving he should not worry about us at all.

This was the dilemma I had been facing for 10 days; I did not say these things when I went to see Pappa as I feared that hearing this, Pappa might give up and the doctors had told me that the willpower and the instinct of living would play a big role for him to recover.

Jay, the grandson of Pappa, performed the last rites including immersing his last remains. The arrangement with Sangita, which originally was planned for only three months, is now more than thirty years old. And from a long time back, Sangita and Jayendra are not cook and driver for us, and Jay, of course, is the "Grandson of Pappa and Mummy."

Jayendra, Sangita, Jay, and Nandini are an extension of Pappa's family. Jay and Nandini are taking care of us by not only helping us to solve our day-to-day problems but also giving us company and keeping us in good humour.

Shubhani, Maulik, and I took solace from the fact that till Pappa was hospitalised he was fully fit, physically as well mentally and barring from the period of about 21 days when he was in the hospital, never had to take support from anybody. We are also happy that we three could do slightly better than what was expected and both of them witnessed our progress in life. And when they left, they in a way were in a more comfortable state of mind because the problems which were worrying them for so many years were either not there or the intensity of the same had reduced drastically.

On Pappa's first death anniversary, Maulik wrote a note

A giant among men – literally and figuratively!!

The man who faced every challenge life threw at him with a smile and a calm mind.

Challenges that would have broken the spirit of even the strongest person, failed to wipe the smile off his face.

A man who could be a child with a child, an adult with an adult.

A warm, loving human being, he created bon homie and pervading feeling of joy wherever he went.

He lived a rich, full life. Desirous to learn new things till the end, he picked up a crayon for the first time at the age of 85 and created more than 100 paintings in a span of 18 months.

A life worth celebrating. A life that was inspirational to say the least.

*On March 11, 2022, the light went out of that life. And yet, as he himself said **"to live in the hearts of people we leave behind is not to Die."***

He lives on in the hearts of the people who he has left behind.

That is our greatest tribute to him.

On 1st June 2023, a Bolt from the Blue - complete injustice - I call it CRUELTY

"He is known as ALMIGHTY" he untimely snatched away "Maulik" from Shubhani and me.

Every year two college friends of Maulik used to organise a trip to Lonavala. Maulik would come to Mumbai and his friends and their families then would go to Lonavala for a few days. After coming back from Lonavala, Maulik would stay with me for about four days. This was his break for a week from his routine.

On June 1, 2023, he started at 9:00 a.m. in the morning to come to Mumbai by car. Jayendra and Sangita were in the front seats and Maulik was sitting at the back. They had reached Vapi and were going to take a break and have their lunch at Woodland Hotel. My driver was waiting for them at Woodland Hotel. From there, he would bring Maulik to Mumbai in my car. They were less than one km away from the Woodland Hotel when the tragedy struck. The car went up on the divider and banged with an electricity pole. The impact must have been very strong. Maulik perhaps hit the front seat and fell unconscious.

Jayendra and Sangita were also injured but it was not that bad. Jayendra called me at about 1.45 p.m. and said that the car had met with an accident. My first feeling was that as Jayendra himself had called up, it might not be serious. They took Maulik to the hospital which was very nearby by lifting him on the seat of the car. Once they reached, the first doctor examined him and called me up. He said that Maulik was severely injured and they would not be able to operate on him at Vapi. I said, "No problem, we will take him to either Vadodara or Mumbai." Then another doctor called up and told me that it looked like there was no head injury as he regained consciousness. This news raised my hope, but then again after a few minutes, another doctor called me up and said he was not breathing normally. I said, "It is possible because he has asthma and that may be the reason." Then another doctor called up to say that things were difficult as his blood pressure was getting low. This according to him was possible only because of internal injuries.

Till that moment, I was refusing to believe that the problem was severe. After about half an hour, another doctor called up and said his heart had failed and they were trying to revive him. Throughout this period, I was constantly in touch with Shubhani and was updating her about the status.

Then the HELL BROKE. The doctor called up and said, "HE IS NO MORE."

In my life, I have never felt so helpless, so angry and so frustrated. When I called up Shubhani to inform her about this devastating news, her first reaction was, "આવો જુલમ કોઈ કરી શકે આપણી ઉપર?" (*"Can anyone be so cruel to us?"*)

We were so numb that neither she nor I could even cry. It just did not register. For me, even after a period of one year, it is still the same, it is still not getting digested. The wound is not healing.

Immediately after the accident, we were also concerned about the formalities. Vapi was an unknown place for us, but approximately in 20 minutes, about six people who were either a relative or a friend or a colleague of our neighbour or relative or a friend reached the hospital. These were the people who could give comfort to me and Shubhani about formalities that would follow post-accident. I, along with my friends, was about to leave for Vapi but people over there called me up and told me that I need not come to Vapi. They assured me that they would handle everything and take care of all the formalities.

I and Shubhani will always remain indebted to all the persons who took care of everything at Vapi and ensured that all formalities were completed on the same day and Maulik came to Vadodara at 2.30 a.m. at night.

In Vadodara again everything was arranged at the hospital for Maulik at night as the cremation could take place only on the next day. This arrangement was also done without any effort from Shubhani or me.

This is not the first car accident in the world, but my complaint is that when it came to giving life, we did not get the same life which everybody else got. We had to fight for everything and this fight was not only for a day, it was every day and when it came to taking away, we were treated like everybody else.

So bright, such a wonderful person, such a fighter and this is how one treats Maulik and this is how one treats Shubhani and me? NOT ACCEPTABLE.

As Ghalib has put it "यही है आज़माना, तो फ़िर सताना किसको कहते हैं?" *(Yehi hai Aazmana to fir Satana kisko kehte hai?") Just because we never complained about the difficult times and always lived joyfully, does not mean that we are not hurt.*

People say that time heals but perhaps this injustice, I will never forget or forgive, never ever.

As Javed Akhtar has put it in one of his shers, where he says, "आसुदगी से दिल के सभी दाग धुल गए, लेकिन वो कैसे जाए जो शीशे में बाल है" *(Aasudgi is a state of mind when you are not worried, are now really flourishing and you have a lot of money, lot of wealth). [Prosperity can heal old wounds, but those which have bruised our soul.]*

When I was going through the drawers of Maulik to look for important documents, I found a writing pad. It was new and in that, Maulik had written a note for Jay. This was surprising because Jay and Nandini were coming home to meet Maulik and Shubhani at least twice a week and whenever they would come, they would have dinner and would spend a good amount of time with them. Then why Maulik wrote a note to Jay was surprising and the content of the note gave a real shock. On reading the words that he has used in his note, one gets a feeling that Maulik was expecting something to happen and that is why this note.

Dear Jay,

I write this to you to let you know that you will find this world an unfair place many times in your life. The key is to accept that it is so, and taking that as given, do the best that you can with your ability and resources.

There will also be a temptation to take the easy way out of tough situations. That is something you will come to regret later in your life.

Meet the challenges head-on but at the same time choose your battles wisely. Remember, not every battle is worth fighting for and not all battles need to be run away from.

I hope that when I move on, people will say "Here was a man who met life on his own terms and did the best he could" If I can leave behind a spirit of "can do" in the weakest person, I would have lived my life to the fullest.

Maulik

The Day After…

We lost Maulik on 1st June; we saw him off on 2nd June. We actually did not see him. He came wrapped in black plastic and we were advised not to open it to see him. We should remember his face the way we had seen him - always smiling.

Apart from other things, one thing which was weighing very heavily on my mind was his company. Personally, I wanted it to continue as that company was his dream.

On 4th June, I and his two associates (they happen to be our nephews) who are attached to this company for more than a decade sat down to discuss the possibility of continuing the company. After discussing at length, the three of us were clear that we would continue.

On 5th June, we wrote to our clients that we wished to continue and whatever Maulik had committed would be fulfilled by us. After that, they could decide about the future course of action.

I was staying alone in Mumbai for thirty years. I shifted to Vadodara in a way on 2nd June.

People feel that I have shifted to Vadodara to take care of Shubhani. It is the other way around; I have shifted so that she can take care of me. She is actually the pillar of strength.

Jay, like for Pappa, performed the last rites and along with Nandini went to Varanasi for immersing his last remains. He went to Varanasi as Maulik had told him that once he would like to visit Varanasi.

No words are enough to thank our relatives, friends including their wives and children, neighbours of Mumbai, and the senior-most persons of the company where we all worked, for helping us to get up and for holding our hand till we stabilised. Normally, they say that out of sight is out of mind, but unlike that, we have a very strong bonding with all of them and they take very good care of us. Shubhani and I will always remain indebted to them for their help, love, and affection.

A lot of people came personally or called up to console Shubhani and me. When they talked to us, it looked like even they were also going through the same amount of pain and their words of consolation really helped Shubhani and me to go through that difficult time.

I must admit that Shubhani has faced this situation with a lot of maturity. After the prayer meeting, Shubhani wrote a note to express gratitude to each and everybody for helping us to go through this most difficult time.

She wrote:

"જહોન મિલ્ટને જ્યારે આંખો ગુમાવી, ત્યારે એણે એક કવિતા લખી. – પેરેડાઈઝ લોસ્ટ.

પહેલી જૂનની બપોરે અમે પણ અમારી જિંદગીનો સિતારો ગુમાવી દીધો.

પરંતુ, પપ્પાએ અમને એક વસ્તુ હંમેશાં શીખવાડી છે કે બાજીમાં જે પત્તાં આવ્યાં, એનાંથી જ જીતવાનો પ્રયત્ન કરવાનો.

આ એક્સિડન્ટ પછી જે મુશ્કેલીઓ આવી શકે, એમાંથી અમારે બિલકુલ પસાર ન થવું પડ્યું.

એમાં કેટલીક એવી વ્યક્તિઓ હતી, જેમને અમે કોઈ દિવસ મળ્યાં પણ નથી.

એમની મદદ માટે અમે એમને સલામ કરીએ છીએ.

તમે બધાંએ, એ વિકટ પરિસ્થિતિમાં જે મદદ કરી, અમને કળ વળે, ત્યાં સુધી જે હૂંફ આપી, એને માટે 'આભાર' શબ્દ બહુ ટૂંકો પડે છે.

એ જ કવિની બીજી કવિતા હતી – પેરેડાઈઝ રિગેઇન્ડ.

તમારા સાથ અને સહકારથી અમે આ દુ:ખમાંથી ઊભાં થઈ જઈશું, એવો અમને વિશ્વાસ છે.

મૌલિક જિંદગી સાથે લડ્યો અને એની શરતો પર જીવ્યો.

એનો શોક ન કરાય, એના પ્રયત્નને ફક્ત બિરદાવી શકાય.

એ દાદ, એ જ એ સિતારાને અંજલિ."

[Summary in English:

'Paradise Lost', a famous poetry was written by John Milton when he lost his eyesight.

We lost an apple of our eye on June 1.

But we have been taught by our father that we must try to win with whatever cards we have in our hands.

Such accident brings many hassles apart from actual loss. We were spared from all those inconveniences.

And it was due to the efforts of some of those persons whom we had never met in our life.

We salute them for their kind gesture.

The word 'Thank you' sounds too incapable of reflecting our gratitude to all those who stood by us in our most difficult times.

The same poet had written another poetry – 'Paradise Regained'. We have the faith that with your help, we will soon gather ourselves out of this.

Maulik fought gallantly with every challenge and lived his life on his terms.

We should not mourn his death. Such life should be celebrated.

A wholehearted commendation for his attempt to face life is the real tribute to him.]

Reflections and Legacy

Yashashchandra Family Foundation

We all very strongly believe that whatever little three of us could achieve in life was mainly because of the help that we got from society and now we should pay back to society. Keeping that objective in mind, we have created a foundation whose objective is to help those students who are physically challenged but are ready to fight with the circumstances. This foundation will help them to pay their fees.

This foundation will also take up the expenses of any institution, which it will incur to create an infrastructure that will help physically challenged students to attend classes.

On the Birthday of Maulik (4th of July 2023), fees were paid to TWO students from this foundation. One student is doing his MBBS at Vadodara and the other one is doing his Computer Engineering from Anand.

This humble intent with which the foundation is created is again a small gesture from all five of us and with full knowledge that even after this, whatever we got from society can never be paid back in totality.

One can contact us at www.yff.org.in

A Personal Note

I must say over here that it is not that we did not feel low on a few occasions, but then it was one or the other family member or a friend who would cheer us up and convince us that there is nothing to worry. The problems were so many that we followed the technique of focusing on solving the immediate problems and for problems of the future, it was always "we will cross that bridge when we come to it."

We never allowed somebody else to decide what we can do and what we can't because we always believed that we are the best judge of our strengths and shortcomings. We definitely took advice, but it was we who decided whether to follow that advice or not.

Our approach towards any particular goal was not to find reasons for "WHY WE CAN NOT DO IT" but "WHAT SHOULD WE DO SO THAT WE CAN DO IT."

We are never ashamed of seeking help, but we seek help only when it is needed. To give an example: "Up to a particular year I never asked for a wheelchair at the airport," or we ask someone to hold our hand only when it is really needed and leave it immediately once we have crossed the hurdle.

We always believe that if we try our best, then seeing our effort, somebody will certainly come up and help us. We never forget to say THANK YOU to the person who has helped, it could be even to a small kid, and that THANK YOU is from the bottom of our hearts.

The real game changers in the life of the three of us were the positive attitude of Pappa and Mummy, their love and affection, and their indefatigable faith in our abilities. An equally important role was played by our relatives, friends, neighbours, teachers, professors, colleagues, employers, and by so many strangers who went out of their way to help and boost our confidence.

I would like to reiterate humbly that this book is written only to convey to people who at times may feel that **"they have not got a fair deal"** and **"Why me?"** and resultantly either give up on life or become people with negative thoughts that perhaps they are in a much better position than what Pappa and Mummy were. To showcase what a wonderful change in life can be brought about with a strong faith in humanity. And to assure families and their differently-abled child that they need not be afraid to DREAM BIG and that with positive thinking, best effort, and a spirit of **"can do,"** you can surely fulfil your dreams.

As Maulik used to say, *"Know your limitations but never allow them to limit your dreams and ambitions."*

The title of this book was given by Maulik and originally it was he who was to write this autobiography. But he had just finished the "PREFACE" when tragedy struck. I was so disgusted with the incident of Maulik being snatched away from us that for a few days, I had given up on the idea of this book.

But then I decided that I must try to complete everything he had started. I am very sure that had he written this book, it definitely would have been much more interesting and a better experience for the reader. Accepting it without even the slightest doubt, I am happy that I could at least complete the book. I am thankful to Shubhani, Shaishav Mehta, Nishi Doshi, Kishore Saletore, Prarthan Desai, and Khyati Kharod for their valuable feedback and suggestions.

Shakti Mehta

Author Bio

I am Shakti Mehta, a Chartered Accountant by qualification. I retired in November 2022 as Vice President (Finance and Accounts) of a multinational company. Over my 37 years of experience, I had the chance to take on various important assignments and I'm glad I could deliver good results.

Currently, I manage Infinity Consultants Limited, a company my younger brother Maulik started, which focuses on management consultancy for small and medium enterprises. I've always had a love for music, and after retiring, I finally started learning it. I also enjoy travelling, and despite my physical challenges, I've managed to travel quite a bit.

I hope this book connects with readers and serves the purpose it is meant for.